Joseph Cheal

Practical Fruit-growing

Joseph Cheal

Practical Fruit-growing

ISBN/EAN: 9783337106577

Printed in Europe, USA, Canada, Australia, Japan

Cover: Foto ©ninafisch / pixelio.de

More available books at **www.hansebooks.com**

PRACTICAL
FRUIT-GROWING

BY

J. CHEAL, F.R.H.S.,

*Member of Fruit Committee Roy. Hort. Society; Member of Executive Committee
British Fruit Growers' Association; Member Committee of Experts
of the Fruiterers' Company, etc.*

ILLUSTRATED

LONDON: GEORGE BELL & SONS,
YORK STREET, COVENT GARDEN.
AND NEW YORK.
1893

PREFACE.

THIS volume, which is a reprint of the first part of the author's larger work on " Fruit Culture," has been issued mainly with a view to meeting the requirements of the numerous agricultural classes which the County Councils are organizing throughout the country. The author's aim has been to give such clear and practical instruction as may help to popularize the subject of which it treats, which has been too long neglected in this country.

CONTENTS.

		PAGE
CHAP. I.—GENERAL PROSPECTS OF CULTURE FOR PROFIT	.	1
,, II.—SELECTION OF SOIL AND SITUATION		10
,, III.—PREPARATION OF GROUND	.	23
,, IV.—WHAT TO PLANT		28
,, V.—PLANTING.	.	40
,, VI.—PRUNING	.	55
,, VII.—COST AND RETURNS PER ACRE . . .	,	62
,, VIII.—RENOVATING OLD ORCHARDS . . . ,	.	66
,, IX.—GATHERING, PACKING, AND DISTRIBUTING .	.	73
,, X.—STORING, PRESERVING, ETC.	.	82
,, XI.—GRAFTING, BUDDING, AND STOCKS . . .	.	97

FRUIT CULTURE.

CHAPTER I.

GENERAL PROSPECTS OF CULTURE FOR PROFIT.

As we have been passing through a time of agricultural depression, when wheat-growing has ceased to be the profitable occupation that it once was, and as there is no prospect of a return to the old prices, it behoves all cultivators of land to consider what other means may be adopted in the way of producing other crops that will be likely to yield a more satisfactory return.

One of the directions in which cultivators may turn to realize this is that of fruit culture.

We are at the present time, as a nation, consuming enormous quantities of fruit, the supply of which comes very largely from abroad, and of kinds that could be grown at home. Here, then, is a large standing order for a commodity that might be produced by our own cultivators, our own land, and our own labour, but which we are quietly allowing the foreigner to supply.

Farmers, as a rule, are not in a hurry to turn from the beaten track and to try experiments in new directions; and frequently the chances and opportunities in this respect are against them.

Want of full knowledge of the subject, the need of

altered conditions of tenancy, and matters of this kind have caused the farmer to stand still in this matter of fruit culture; and while he has been hesitating, a few of the more adventurous ones, with better opportunities, have been going ahead.

With the large increase of population and the prosperity of the people, the demand for fruit has enormously increased, and how has it been met? A comparatively few keen, far-sighted cultivators have certainly risen to the occasion, and have been providing for this demand by planting and cultivating quantities of high-class fruit; but the supply has been altogether inadequate to the demand. This has opened the way to our cousins across the water; and the American growers, and our own colonists in Canada, have not been slow to seize the opportunity of supplying our wants.

Our own cultivators, or rather possessors of orchards which have to a great extent been uncultivated, are in the meantime crying out that they cannot sell the apples that they already grow; but the reason of this is not far to seek. The apples sent to market from these orchards will be found in most cases to be such a mixture that the housewife can find amongst them any sort except the ones she needs, and they appear to have had in gathering the treatment by the farmer that Talpa recommended him to give to his clods, in the old book "The Chronicles of a Clay Farm":—

> "Mingle, mingle, mingle, all ye who mingle may,
> Blue spirits and white, black spirits and grey."

This treatment is all right for the clods, but all wrong for the apples.

The American orchardists have seen their opportunity, and taken it. They have noted the requirements of our markets and have set themselves to work to meet those requirements, and they have by careful study and scientific practice been able to produce and place upon our markets, thousands and tens of thousands of bushels of apples of good quality, especially handsome in appearance, regular in size, and uniform in quality. These find ready sale, not only in large cities, but also in our provincial towns, and even in our country villages, at the very doors of those who could grow just as good themselves, and who are perhaps complaining of bad times, and the hopelessness of making corn growing pay.

But the responsibility for this state of things is by no means confined to the farmer, the lethargy of the landowners with respect to this matter is unaccountable. They have been standing still with their tenants, and supplying themselves with fruit from across the water, instead of from their own lands.

Apples that can be produced of such handsome appearance and placed on our markets in such fine condition are sure to sell, and people will continue to buy until we can supply them with a sufficient quantity of better fruit at home. And that the quality of our fruit, of the best varieties, when grown with care and scientific skill, is superior to that from over the water is abundantly proved by the much higher price invariably realized for such fruit. Highly coloured skins do not always indicate the highest quality inside, and most of the American fruits are dry and woolly compared with the juicy lusciousness of our own prime English fruit. The moral obviously is, that those who grow the fruit must produce the highest quality. The fruit must be *cultivated*, and not allowed simply to *grow*.

That a movement has set in in this direction is very

evident, as shown by the agricultural returns of fruit planted in this country, which exhibit an increase during the last two years to the extent of 12,000 acres, as against a decrease in the year previous of 500 acres; so that pessimists are beginning to say, "Ah, yes! now it will be overdone"; but there is no prospect or possibility of this for many years to come. With the increase of supplies of good fruit, the consumption will extend enormously, and the supply will create further demand. As a proof of this, take the case of tomatoes. The consumption of these twenty years ago was confined to a very limited number, but now that people have become educated to their use, and have discovered their wholesome qualities, they are in daily demand by the million, and their growth has probably increased a hundred-fold during that period. An interesting calculation in the *Country Gentleman*, an American organ, as to the quantity of fruit that might and ought to be consumed by the people is given as follows:—

"Each member of every family should have, on an average, one pound of fruit daily—some will eat more, some less—either fresh or cooked. How many pounds will that be in each day? There are 40,000,000 persons in the whole country old enough or well enough to eat fruit, which would be 40,000,000 lbs. or nearly 20,000 tons daily consumption. Taking the year through, it would amount to 7,000,000 tons. The daily consumption of fruit would prevent many persons from eating or imbibing what is much worse, and at the same time it would contribute greatly to health, and prevent disease. We want more enterprise, skill, calculation, and management to raise and properly distribute these 7,000,000 tons."

What we should require at the same rate of consumption on this side the water may be ascertained when the census returns are issued.

Those who enter upon fruit culture must not, however, expect to make fortunes in a year. Much has been said and written which is wide of the truth as to profits —so wide, indeed, that it does much harm instead of good. Exaggeration and over-statement only weaken the argument and raise suspicion, and ultimately lead to disappointment, in those who listen to and act upon it. But there is abundant proof that those who plant carefully, and cultivate with common sense, to say nothing of scientific skill, reap a fair return for their outlay and labour. This is proved, not merely by large growers for market, but by a considerable number of small cultivators.

Many persons seeing this, and desiring to enter upon fruit culture upon a larger or smaller scale, are seeking reliable information and guidance as to the best methods of proceeding, and this requires much thought and careful consideration. Do not hastily rush into it, but consider well the general prospects, and especially whether there is any particular advantage or inducement in your own case. For instance, whether you have in your possession or occupation land that is suitable to the purpose, whether you have any special means of disposing of the fruit, and all considerations of a like kind. Then, according to your circumstances and surroundings, determine upon your course of action. Many points will have to be thought out and determined before even commencing. There will be the question of whether you have a retail outlet for your fruit, or whether it must be sent to a wholesale market, whether you would be likely to get a better return for early or late varieties, and whether you have a jam factory or other means of disposing of the fruit.

All these considerations would have a bearing upon the varieties to plant, and upon the general arrangement.

These points being determined by the intending grower, he should then select his position accordingly, or if this is already fixed, he will determine his action from his surroundings. Then let him steadily pursue his purpose, and not be daunted or turned from it by the first or second failure; but having made sure that he is on the right course, go steadily ahead.

To those who may be contemplating fruit growing, who may not have much practical acquaintance with the subject, I would remind them of the words "in the multitude of counsellors is safety," but on the other hand the more homely saying equally applies, that "too many cooks spoil the broth." In other words, hear all sides, get all the advice that you can, weigh the evidence, arrange your plans, and then proceed according to your own judgment and common sense.

Do not imagine that success is gained by merely careful preparation and planting, but ever bear in mind that fruit trees require vigilant watching, as to their varied needs, according to seasons and soils, and the ravages of insect pests. But where this vigilance, common sense, and persevering labour are bestowed upon fruit culture, it will be found a safe and profitable industry.

One great drawback to fruit culture in the past has been the time that must necessarily elapse after planting before realizing a return. According to the old methods, it was useless to expect anything like a profitable return from fruit trees for at least ten to twelve years after planting. Modern science and practice have, however, done much to alter this. Necessity in this case, as in many others, has stimulated invention, and by the use of dwarfing stocks and other similar means almost a revolution in fruit culture has been accomplished. Many of our apples for which we had to wait years for a crop, by

Fig. 1.—Apples on Tree, three years old, on Paradise Stock.

working on the paradise stock will now yield fruit the second season after grafting; and what the paradise has done for the apple, the quince has done for the pear.

What was said of the pear, according to the old lines, is now changed into the following:—

> "That 'Those who plant pears
> Grow fruit for their heirs,'
> Is a maxim our grandfathers knew.
> But folks have learned since,
> If you graft on the quince,
> The fruit will develop for you."

Another great drawback has undoubtedly been our system of land tenure. This has by no means favoured, and in numberless instances has precluded, tenants from entering upon fruit culture to any extent. Without special arrangements with his landlord, the ordinary tenant indeed cannot do so. If he were to, he would have to expend a considerable sum upon what he could not remove on leaving, and his landlord might object to pay for it. There have been in recent years Acts of Parliament passed to protect the tenant farmer, and to give compensation for unexhausted improvements; but this does not seem to apply with sufficient force in the case of the planting of fruit trees to adequately protect the tenant, and where there is no special arrangement it may lead to as unpleasant and disastrous a result as that recorded some time since in the *Sussex Advertiser*, as follows:

"LAND TENURE IN KENT.—One of the results of the unsatisfactory system of land tenure now prevailing in this country is to be seen at Knockholt, Kent. The lease held by Mr. Edwin Bath, of Curry Farm, in that parish, expires at Michaelmas, and he is not allowed to renew his tenancy, nor can he recover compensation from his landlord for a valuable plantation of raspberries on the farm. Consequently, the extraordinary spectacle may now be seen of a reaping machine cutting down, and a steam plough following it rooting up this plantation, which has cost a very large expenditure of time and money to produce. When it is considered that the produce of the plantation in question realized in the present year upwards of £1,690, and that the plantation was vigorous and in full bearing, some idea may be formed of the sacrifice of property involved."

In some cases the landlord will agree to pay the value of a plantation at the expiration of the tenancy; but if fruit be planted to any large extent, compensation at the termination of a long lease might mean such a serious matter, that a landlord may well hesitate before committing himself or his heirs to such a heavy and uncertain charge.

The most satisfactory arrangement seems to be for the landlord to find the trees, and the tenant to find the labour, and prepare the ground for planting. It is, of course, to their mutual interest to select good trees of the right varieties, and to plant and cultivate them properly. It is also especially to the interest of the tenant to maintain and cultivate them well, in order to realize the best return from them in the shortest possible time, and he will be naturally anxious to continue his tenancy as long as possible in order to reap the full benefit of his first outlay; and the landlord is thus likely to secure a good thriving tenant, and to see his property considerably increasing in value. There is then at the expiration of the tenancy no vexed question respecting valuation and compensation.

An instance came under my notice a short time since of a landlord who some years ago expended about £20 an acre in planting apples for a tenant, upon land which previously let for £1 per acre. The land has now for many years been let at £4 per acre, whilst the land adjoining is still let for £1 per acre. Therefore the £20 outlay in planting fruit has yielded to the landlord £3 per annum, which is not a bad interest on the outlay, to say nothing of the largely increased capital value. I think, if carefully looked at from a landlord's point of view, it will be seen that it is not only the duty, but the interest of landlords to give every facility that they legitimately can to good tenants as regards this matter of fruit culture

CHAPTER II.

SELECTION OF SOIL AND SITUATION.

To those about to embark in fruit culture, the first step, and one of great importance, is the selection of soil and a suitable situation. The soil upon which fruit may be profitably grown is more varied than is often supposed. This is pretty clearly shown by the way that fruit trees thrive in kitchen gardens and cottage gardens in almost all parts of the country. The soil, even where originally considered uncongenial, has been made suitable by good and constant cultivation, and the application of manure.

Generally speaking, the land selected, if choice be open, should be naturally rich, a good strong loam, with a fairly porous subsoil. Kent undoubtedly has the pre-eminence as affording the best fruit-growing land in the country, but many other counties possess soil and positions little inferior to it in quality. The deep rich red land of Herefordshire, Devon, and Somerset; the lias and the limestone of Worcestershire and Gloucestershire, and the lighter clays and the Hastings sands of Sussex; the rich alluvial soils of Middlesex, Cambridge, and Lincolnshire, are all adapted to the cultivation of fruit, and large breadths of fruit plantations and orchards are found in each.

Acreage of Orchards and Small Fruits in England, 1890.

County.	Orchards. Apples, Pears, Plums, Cherries, etc.	Small Fruits. Gooseberries, Currants, Raspberries, and Strawberries.	Totals Combined.
	Acres.	Acres.	Acres.
Bedford	719	166	885
Berks	2,367	188	2,555
Buckingham	2,447	268	2,715
Cambridge	2,370	1,727	4,097
Chester	1,918	1,185	3,103
Cornwall	5,045	957	6,002
Cumberland	306	179	485
Derby	1,018	403	1,421
Devon	26,587	1,005	27,592
Dorset	4,319	10	4,420
Durham	282	263	545
Essex	1,578	725	2,303
Gloucester	16,619	926	17,545
Hants	1,702	1,130	2,832
Hereford	25,991	184	26,175
Hertford	1,306	300	1,606
Huntingdon	554	303	857
Kent	18,168	15,329	33,497
Lancaster	2,461	1,794	4,255
Leicester	972	351	1,323
Lincoln	1,942	1,013	2,955
Middlesex	3,944	2,831	6,775
Monmouth	3,888	74	3,962

FRUIT CULTURE.

County.	Orchards. Apples, Pears, Plums, Cherries, etc. Acres.	Small Fruits. Gooseberries, Currants, Raspberries, and Strawberries. Acres.	Totals Combined. Acres.
Norfolk ...	2,252	1,173	3,425
Northampton ...	722	235	957
Northumberland	114	401	515
Notts ...	1,872	585	2,457
Oxford ...	1,737	109	1,846
Rutland ...	72	53	125
Salop ...	4,026	146	4,172
Somerset ...	24,048	362	24,410
Stafford ...	1,249	150	1,399
Suffolk ...	1,708	449	2,157
Surrey ...	2,252	868	3,120
Sussex ...	2,525	795	3,320
Warwick ...	1,839	321	2,160
Westmoreland ...	351	39	390
Wilts ...	3,383	116	3,499
Worcester ...	19,252	1,639	20,891
York, East Riding	730	669	1,399
„ North Riding	917	374	1,291
„ West Riding	1,524	1,195	2,719
Totals ...	197,076	41,081	238,157

In selecting the most suitable position, it is necessary to bear in mind what line of culture is desired, and what particular fruit or fruits are intended to be grown, and this will greatly help to determine the soil and locality. Some of the considerations that would help to settle this are, for instance, whether fruits are to be grown principally for dessert purposes, and to be gathered and sent to market from the orchard, or whether apples and pears are to be stored for winter use, or whether the fruit is to be grown for a factory. In each case different soils and situations might be selected. All these matters should receive careful consideration, and the ultimate *object* should be kept steadily in view in order to *start* right. Upon this point science is of the utmost value to cultivators. A correct analysis of the character and constituent parts of each particular variety of fruit indicates the nature of the soil required to sustain it; and, on the other hand, an analysis of the soil shows what kind of tree will thrive best upon it in its natural condition, and will also be found of the greatest assistance in applying manures, enabling the cultivator to supply the ingredients that may be deficient in the soil.

We will now glance at the particular soils that seem best suited to each kind of fruit, in order that the planter may be able to judge as to what soil would best answer his purpose, or if he already possesses soil, as to what fruits would be most suitable for him to grow.

APPLES.—A light or heavy loam, subsoil clay; or chalk if there is 3 or 4 ft. of soil overlying it. They should not be planted upon low or wet situations or too near to rivers or large bodies of water, neither on high and exposed situations.

PEARS.—On pear stock, light loam, subsoil gravel; on quince stock, light to heavy loam, subsoil clay.

PLUMS.—Light sandy loam, subsoil light clay or gravel; or they will do well upon a chalk subsoil if there is a good depth of strong loamy soil upon the surface.

CHERRIES.—Good loam, overlying chalk.

FILBERTS and COBS.—A good porous loam; and they will

often do well upon banks where the ground is somewhat rocky, also in shady situations and northern slopes.

CURRANTS.—A wide range of soils from light to heavy loam, subsoil clay or gravel; and black currants may be planted on heavy land, which is somewhat low and wet.

GOOSEBERRIES.—Rich sandy loam, subsoil gravel.

RASPBERRIES.—A light sandy loam, subsoil gravel; or heavier loam if the subsoil be open.

STRAWBERRIES.—A wide range of soils. A good rich loam is the best, either upon gravel, or clay if not too cold; and they also do well upon chalk if there is a moderate layer of surface mould.

SOILS AND THEIR COMPOSITION.

Soils perform at least three functions in reference to the growth and culture of fruit trees. In the first place, they serve as a basis in which the trees may fix their roots, and sustain themselves in an erect position. Secondly, they supply food to the trees at each period of their growth. And thirdly, they are the medium in which many chemical changes take place that are essential to the suitable preparation of the various elements of plant food, which the soil is destined to yield to the growing tree, for the production of stem, foliage, flowers and fruit. In fact, a fertile soil may well be described as a laboratory, as well as a mine.

From numerous investigations and ascertained facts in relation to soils, certain important deductions in regard to fruit growing may safely be drawn.

It may be too much to say that a fruit tree will not grow in a soil that is destitute of nitrogen, but at the same time it may certainly be affirmed that no profitable crop of fruit can be grown unless the soil itself, or the manure which is applied, contains nitrogen.

That substances rich in nitrogen increase the verdure, darken the foliage-colour, and generally promote and prolong the growth of the trees is a recognised fact.

Lime is found in all fertile soils, and, indeed, it enters into the composition of every kind of plant and animal. And experience teaches us that it forms a very necessary element in all successful fruit growing, and more especially in the production of stone fruit. In its more common form it tends to strengthen the stem and woody portion of the tree, generally shortens the period of growth, and hastens the time of ripening.

Hence we find that retentive clays that contain little or no lime in their composition extend the period of growth and ripening, with the result that some of the strong growing varieties do not properly mature their wood or ripen their fruit, and are most easily affected by frost.

On the other hand, in a shallow, moderately light soil, say from fifteen to twenty inches deep, which rests upon a subsoil of chalk, marl, or loose rock, the growth of a fruit tree will be moderate, the shoots short and sturdy, and the fruit well ripened.

A careful examination of the most successful vineyards and fruit orchards on the Continent will show that the greater part of the soil consists of argil-calcareous or argillaceous gravel.

The vineyards of the Rhine are all planted upon thin soils, with rocky foundations, but sparingly covered with soil.

Composition of Soils.

The following particulars as to the constituents of Californian soils may be of interest.

	Adobe Soil, 12 to 22 inches deep. Per cent.	Adobe Subsoil, 22 to 30 inches deep. Per cent.
Loam	47·6	23·4
Clay	31·9	33·5
Gravel	20·5	43·1
Total	100·0	100·0
Organic matter	5·72	6·60
Lime	1·05	0·99
Potash	0·45	0·10
Soda	0·07	0·10
Magnesia	1·21	1·91
Phosphoric acid	0·23	0·11
Iron oxide	4·67	7·29

The high percentage of iron oxide as shown above, is probably the chief contributing cause of the brightness in colour of the Californian fruits.

We will now give some analyses of English soils, by the late Dr. Volcker, as affording good examples of the more frequent and important varieties of soil in the British Isles, adding such remarks as may appear applicable to each.

1. COMPOSITION OF A CALCAREOUS CLAYEY SURFACE SOIL.

Selected Constituents in 100 parts.

	Per cent.		Per cent.
Organic matter	11·08	Lime	11·53
Clay	52·06	Potash	0·32
Sand	24·53	Phosphoric acid	0·12

Such a soil for fruit growing requires only to be kept up to its present condition of fertility, which may be done by giving an occasional dressing of good stable manure, say from ten to twenty tons per acre, and bringing it into play by an application of from one to two cwts. nitrate of soda per acre, whilst for the purpose of giving colour to the fruit add one cwt. sulphate of iron every second year.

2. Composition of a Fertile Loam.

Selected Constituents in 100 parts.

	Surface Soil. Per cent.	Subsoil. Per cent.
Organic matter	4·38	2·59
Clay	18·09	41·79
Sand	76·16	55·15
Lime	1·37	0·47
Potash	0·49	0·88
Phosphoric acid	0·12	0·19

This soil, which contained a little lime intermixed with the clay subsoil upon which it rested, with abundance of potash and phosphoric acid, might be kept up in fertility by an application of stable manure or compost, to which might be added a mixture composed of 3 cwts. superphosphate of lime, 2 cwts. nitrate of soda or sulphate of ammonia, and 1 cwt. sulphate of iron.

3. Composition of a Heavy Tenacious Clay.

Selected Constituents in 100 parts.

	Surface Soil. Per cent.	Subsoil. Per cent.
Organic matter	4·87	4·80
Clay	75·29	78·13
Sand	9·26	10·97
Lime	1·15	2.23
Alkalies and magnesia	1·37	0·32
Phosphoric acid	0·06	0·04

This soil, which came from the upper oolite formation, contained but a very small proportion of sand or of phosphoric acid, and would be greatly benefited for fruit growing by a liberal application of old "mortar rubbish," and an occasional dressing of 2 cwts. superphosphate, 2 to 3 cwts. basic slag (ground fine), 1 cwt. muriate of potash, and 1 cwt. of nitrate of soda.

4. Composition of a Sterile Sandy Soil.
Selected Constituents in 100 parts.

	Per cent.
Organic matter	5·36
Clay	4·57
Sand	89·82
Lime	0·25
Alkalies and magnesia.	0·49
Phosphoric acid	a trace.

A plentiful supply of rich stable manure is here required, with about 4 cwt. superphosphate, or 6 cwt. of basic slag, 2 cwt. of muriate of potash, and $1\frac{1}{2}$ cwt. nitrate of soda. And as this soil contains an abundance of sand for draining purposes, a frequent and liberal application of liquid manure may be given.

5. Composition of an Orchard Soil covered with Turf
Selected Constituents in 100 parts.

	Per cent.
Organic matter	11·70
Clay	48·39
Sand	35·95
Lime	1·54
Potash	0·91
Phosphoric acid	0·08

This soil, which may be described as a vegetable mould,

contains abundance of organic matter with a fair proportion of sand and clay, and can therefore be kept in fertility by an occasional dressing of 1½ cwts. superphosphate.

Every ordinary soil, however "worn out" it may be, can do something towards supporting plant life. It does this by virtue of what may be aptly termed its "natural strength." By this is meant the capacity which it has as the resultant of its chemical composition and physical character, previously described, its supply of plant food and moisture, its texture, warmth and so on, for yielding crops of fruit year after year without manure.

This strength accumulated by natural processes, or imparted artificially, is like a deposit in the bank, which we can drawn upon slowly or rapidly at will, but which will, sooner or later be exhausted unless new deposits are made.

Chemical Composition of Fruit and Fruit Trees.

A study of the chemical composition of the wood of various fruit trees, and of the fruit itself, will teach us what is abstracted from the soil by their growth.

Table showing the percentage composition of the wood of various fruit bearing trees.

Selected Constituents in the ashes of 100 parts.

	Potash.	Lime.	Magnesia.	Phosphoric Acid.
Apple	19·2	63·6	7·5	4·9
Pear	4·2	77·2	5·1	3·8
Cherry	20·8	28·7	9·2	7·7
Raspberry	14·2	38·2	10·8	23·6
Walnut	11·3	35·9	3·7	4·1
Chestnut	10·1	43·6	3·2	1·5

The timber of freely growing fruit trees yields when

burnt as fuel but a small proportion of ashes, which on analysis show that there is, besides vegetable matter, a great loss of the mineral constituents of the soil, which will of course be greater, according as the pruning knife is used upon the branches, and the leaves after falling are removed from the land.

The following table shows the percentage composition of the ash or mineral matter of the fruits themselves.

	Potash.	Soda.	Lime.	Magnesia.	Iron.	Phos. Acid.	Sulph. Acid.	Silic
Apple	46·21	14·02	4·87	6·53	0·93	10·89	3·05	2·8
Cherry	51·85	2·19	7·47	5·46	1·98	15·97	5·09	9·0
Damson	45·98	5·66	12·65	8·17	1·19	13·83	2·37	9·2
Gooseberry	38·65	9·92	12·20	5·85	4·56	19·68	5·89	2·5
Strawberry	21·07	28·48	14·21	—	5·89	13·82	3·15	12·0
Chestnut	39·36	21·73	7·84	7·84	1·03	8·25	3·88	2·3
Figs	28·36	26·27	18·91	9·21	1·46	1·30	6·75	5·9
Pears	54·69	8·52	7·98	5·22	1·04	15·20	5·69	1·4
Plums	59·21	0·54	10·04	5·46	3·30	15·10	3·83	2·3

The following table shows the amount of mineral ingredients extracted from the soil by the growth of one ton of different kinds of fruit.

	lbs.
Apples	9·0
Pears	6·7
Cherries	15·0
Plums	13·7
Gooseberries	11·2
Figs	51·5
Walnuts	38·1
Filberts	33·6

It is obvious, therefore, that every ton of fruit contains several pounds of mineral matter, the whole of which is gathered by it, through the roots and branches from the soil.

The following table shows the analysis of the ashes of apples at different stages of growth and different sizes, the quantities of the various ingredients being given in parts per 100.

	Unripe Apples. Per cent.	Ripe Apples. Per cent.	Small Apples. Per cent.
Silica	0.58	1.23	2.16
Ferric oxide	0.47	0.46	2.16
Phosphoric acid	8.96	8.20	8.73
Lime	6.85	5.66	8.85
Magnesia	4.80	4.30	4.76
Potash	54.02	56.74	52.44
Soda	2.10	1.94	2.08
Undetermined	22.22	21.47	20.62

The only ingredients contained in the ash which there is any need of noting, are the phosphoric acid, potash, and lime; for these are the only ones in which the soil is likely to become deficient, and therefore which need to be returned to the land to keep up its fertility.

From the above analysis we find there would be taken from an acre of land yielding 100 bushels of fruit by sample No. 1, 6 lbs. phosphoric acid, $37\frac{1}{2}$ lbs. potash, and $4\frac{3}{4}$ lbs. lime; by sample No. 2, 7 lbs. phosphoric acid, 37 lbs. potash, and $3\frac{1}{2}$ lbs. lime; by sample No. 3, $7\frac{1}{4}$ lbs. phosphoric acid, 43 lbs. potash, and $7\frac{1}{4}$ lbs. lime.

From these facts we learn the importance of thinning fruit as soon as it is of sufficient size, and also that it *costs less* to grow a bushel of *large* and *perfect* apples than it does to grow a bushel of *small* and *inferior fruit.*

It is further evident that to produce good crops of apples for any number of years, the ground, after the trees are planted, must have phosphoric acid, potash, and lime returned to it as well as nitrogen if we wish to keep up production and fertility of the soil.

When we remove crops of fruit we take away the materials they have accumulated and absorbed from the soil. It may take many years of fruit growing on a fertile soil, before the exhaustion and injury arising from the removal of the crops will become manifest; but when injurious results have once become apparent they will not always admit of a speedy remedy.

Now this brings us to another point. This food supply varies, as we have already seen, in different soils. It varies, not only as a whole, but in its different parts. Sometimes one element, sometimes several may be lacking. If so it cannot yield a full crop.

This same variation runs through both natural or inherent strength and condition. You may often take a soil whose natural strength is below the point of profitable production, and by adding a single substance, a phosphate, or nitrate for instance, bring it into profitable condition.

Further, a soil may be so compact that air and moisture cannot get into it to convert the crude materials it contains, nor the roots make their way through to obtain the food that has been made available. It may be so loose and non-retentive that the food-ingredients will escape. It may be so dry that fertilisers will be useless, and the fruit trees wither on it, or so wet and cold as to prevent their growth. But by proper tillage, drainage, and amendment soil-texture may be improved, its powers of holding water and supplying plant food increased, and thus by manuring it may be brought into condition to yield profitable returns for all that is done for it.

The next question very naturally is, what ingredients of plant food are most frequently deficient in our soils for fruit growing? This, of course, can only be ascertained by an analysis of the particular soil in question. Within the last few years considerable advance has been made in the knowledge of all that relates to the application and action of manures; and it is, we fear, too often a subject for regret, that cultivators of orchards suffer from diminished produce and depreciation of land, arising from a want of a due appreciation and application of those principles by the aid of which some other branches of agriculture and horticulture have of late years so much profited.

CHAPTER III.

PREPARATION OF GROUND.

THE suitability or otherwise of land for immediate planting would depend largely upon the cultivation that it had received, as well as to its natural quality; and the combination of the two would determine the kind of preparation required to render it suitable for planting. Probably the first consideration is that of drainage. Be sure that the land is properly drained. Nothing could be worse for fruit trees than to be planted in land the subsoil of which is close and water-logged. There are, of course, many soils that do not require draining. A test as to its nature in this respect may be made in the following way. If on digging to the subsoil you find it porous and perforated by worms, you may conclude that there is sufficient circulation of water and air through it. If, on the other hand, you find the soil close and retentive, with no worm-holes, you may conclude that the land ought to be drained. Pipe-draining is more expensive than the old plan of straw or bushes, but will be found to well repay the extra outlay in the long run. Let me here emphasize the importance of draining. If the land be water-logged, it is impossible for fruit trees to thrive and maintain a healthy condition. They will become mossy and covered with long grey lichen, and subject to canker and many other diseases, and instead of producing good profitable crops, will become so stunted and unhealthy that what fruit is produced will be comparatively worthless.

The operation of draining is so well understood that there is no need here to describe it in detail, but in setting out the drain it is always well to mark out the intended direction of the rows of trees before commencing, and then to place the drains midway between the rows of standard trees. They are then at the farthest distance possible from the roots of the most permanent trees, and should they at any time require attention, they may be opened without damage to the trees.

The next consideration is the breaking up of the land. If it has been used only for ordinary husbandry, it should in the first place be broken up to a greater depth than has hitherto been the case. The best means of accomplishing this would have to be considered and determined according to the extent and local conditions. If the area is but small, it might be best to break it up by hand. But if sufficiently large and open, it may be done at much less expense by a steam cultivator. This implement merely breaks up and stirs the ground, and does not reverse the position of the surface and the subsoil, but merely loosens the land and slightly mixes the two together.

I may here mention the somewhat new implement that we used here three years ago, which gave us satisfaction, —one of Proctor's Steam Diggers (Fig. 2.) The work of this implement is the nearest approach to hand digging that I have seen, and does literally dig the ground with strong steel forks. The only drawback that we found was that it can only be used in dry weather, as the great weight of the engine passing over the land when it is at all wet does more harm than good. But when the land is dry enough to bear the weight without closing the ground, it makes splendid work, breaking up and slightly mixing the subsoil, and throwing it back leaves it in a light and open condition; and it breaks up the subsoil in such a way that an uneven broken bottom is left below the soil, through which water easily escapes. And if it can be dug up for a few weeks before being required for planting, so much the better.

Fig. 2.—Proctor's Steam Digger.

If, however, no steam tackle can be obtained, or there is not sufficient room for its proper use, a good substitute may be found in the use of the subsoil plough. This follows the ordinary plough along each furrow, breaking up the subsoil from 6 to 9 inches below the depth of the ordinary plough. It is best to employ two teams, the first one ploughing a deep ordinary furrow, followed by the second team with the subsoil plough. As to a suitable make of plough to use, we ourselves tried several without getting one exactly to answer our purpose. But we last season had one made as shown by Fig. 3. The

Fig. 3.—Subsoil Plough.

upright peg on the right-hand side of the cutting share we have found to effect all that is required, and it will be seen, on watching the plough in operation, that this peg thoroughly lifts and breaks up the subsoil, thus leaving it in a loose and open condition.

Where there is not, however, sufficient land for either of the foregoing appliances, it may of course be prepared by hand. This should be done by what is ordinarily known as bastard trenching, or the breaking up of the land two spits deep; but in doing this, on no account must the subsoil be brought to the surface, but merely broken up and turned over, turning the next spit of surface soil on to the top of the subsoil thus broken up.

Whether it is intended to plant orchard standard trees alone or mixed plantations, I would strongly urge the advisability of thus moving the whole of the land to an even depth in preference to digging or trenching holes for each tree. If the land be at all stiff and retentive, this digging of single holes is about the worst possible plan that can be adopted, each hole becoming a mere pan or basin to hold water. In this stagnant water the roots and fibres decay, and the tree becomes stunted, cankered, and unhealthy. But in circumstances where this digging of single holes is the only plan that can be adopted— where the land is in grass, and intended to remain so— let the evils alluded to be avoided by arranging some means of draining the water from each hole, such as running a drain between each alternate row of holes, and connecting the holes on either side with the drain.

As to the condition of land best suited for planting, probably that from which a root crop has been taken, after having been well manured for the roots, may be the best of all. The land will then necessarily have been well worked for the roots, and well manured; the residue of the manure will be sufficient for the trees at the time of planting, and will be in the best condition for the newly forming roots to feed upon. But if the planting is to follow a corn crop, it will be naturally in a more exhausted condition, and will require the application of more manure at the time of planting.

One of the most important considerations is to select land that is *clean;* otherwise, if trees are planted upon land encumbered with weeds, and they once get amongst the roots of the trees, great annoyance and expense will be the result for years, and many of the more tenacious weeds cannot afterwards be extracted without injury to the tree.

If the land be in a poor condition, and has been badly cultivated, it will be far better to wait another season before planting, in order to clean and give good preparation, than to attempt to plant it in an unsuitable condition.

In such a case it is therefore best to take a clear summer fallow, to break up the land as described with the cultivator, and keep it well stirred through the summer, applying a good coat of manure in the autumn before planting. This will really involve no loss of time, but a saving in the end, as the great aim in planting should be to get the trees to flourish and subsequently progress without impediment.

CHAPTER IV.

WHAT TO PLANT.

The question that we now arrive at is a very important one, and needs most careful consideration as to all circumstances affecting the case. Some of the points that may influence the decision may be summarized under the following heads :—

1st. The special line of culture.

2nd. The markets within reach, or other means of disposal.

3rd. Whether early or late markets, or both.

4th. Whether growing for jam or other preserve.

5th. The special varieties suitable for the soil and situation.

It will now, I think, be seen what need there is to keep a definite object in view in order to avoid mistakes in starting. Guided by the above conditions, adopt whatever special line seems most likely to succeed in your own particular case. Then study carefully what varieties would best answer that purpose, and meet the special requirements you have in view. If you have any special facility for supplying a retail market, you would probably be able to realize the highest price, and to meet this you would have to plant a considerable number of varieties, and such as would probably extend in use over a lengthened season. If, on the other hand, you should grow for a wholesale or distant market only, it would be better to cultivate but few varieties, so that you would have large quantities of the same kind to deal with at one time. Or, should you be growing for a jam factory or other preserving establishment, you would naturally select varieties that would be best suited to that particular purpose. It will be impossible in the compass of this work to give suitable instructions to meet all cases which may arise, but the following list of varieties will be found a good general one from which selections may be made to answer most of the above requirements.

Standard Apples.

K signifies kitchen; T, table or dessert. The usual season in which they are in use is indicated by the month.

BLENHEIM ORANGE.—K.T. Nov. to Feb. The king of apples when grown as a standard, the large fruits being suitable for kitchen, and the small ones for dessert. The greatest drawback to this variety is the length of time that elapses before it comes into bearing, eight or ten years being the usual period: a long time for this age of speed. But it is a variety that we cannot do without and can afford to wait for, there being plenty of others which step in to supply the gap during the period of probation. Tree, a vigorous grower, with a spreading habit.

Cox's ORANGE PIPPIN.—T. Oct. to Feb. The king of dessert apples, medium in size, rich in colour, juicy in texture, delicious in flavour. There is no apple in the world that can equal it in quality. Tree, a moderate grower, with a spreading habit.

Duchess of Oldenburg.—K. & T. Aug. to Sept. Medium, roundish, oblong, pale yellow, very handsomely streaked with red, and carrying a delicate bloom. Quality fair, an immense and early bearer. The tree, however, does not succeed on all soils, requiring one of a fairly light and porous nature.

Ecklinville Seedling.—K. Sept. to Oct. A large and fine apple, flat and slightly angular, a greenish yellow, and dotted with brown specks, its only fault being that it is very soft and requires careful packing for market. Tree, a vigorous grower, with a somewhat erect habit. Thrives well on heavy soils.

Golden Noble.—K. Oct. to Dec. A large, and, as its name implies, a truly noble apple, round and even in shape, with a beautiful clear yellow skin. Tree a vigorous grower, with a spreading habit.

King of Pippins.—T. Oct. to Jan. Medium, oblong, rich yellow, flushed red. One of our handsomest apples, being a model in outline and colour. The tree is a good grower, and a certain bearer, and one of the best for market purposes.

Norfolk Beefing.—K. Nov. to July. Medium size, round and flattened; colour, a very dull, deep red. Tree, a vigorous grower, with an upright habit. Valuable on account of its extreme lateness.

Pott's Seedling.—K. Aug. to Sept. A large angular-shaped fruit, slightly flattened; skin, pale yellow. A very free cropper, and good quality. Tree, a good grower, with a slightly spreading habit.

Warner's King.—K. Oct. to Dec. A very large and

fine apple, round, and somewhat flattened; skin, pale green. Tree, a vigorous grower, with very large foliage, and, considering the size of the fruit, a free bearer. The tree has a spreading habit.

Wellington.—K. Dec. to April. A large and well-known fruit. One of our most valuable kitchen apples for late use, and, coming in as they do when fruit is scarce, good samples command high prices. Tree of a spreading habit, and fruit in season from November to April, and even later when well kept.

Winter Queening or Ducksbill of Sussex.—T. and K. Nov. to May. A medium-sized, conical fruit, covered with deep crimson. It is grown largely in Sussex, especially by cottagers and small growers, and called by them the Winter and Scarlet Pearmain. The tree has a spreading habit, and crops well. A valuable late apple.

Worcester Pearmain.—T. Aug. to Sept. Medium, conical; colour, deep crimson; quality, only second rate; but it makes up in appearance what it lacks in quality. Being a heavy and certain cropper, and extremely handsome in appearance, it can be highly recommended as an early market variety.

Beyond the foregoing, a supplementary list of other useful varieties may be mentioned as follows :—

Beauty of Kent, Bramley's Seedling, Claygate Pearmain, Dutch Mignonne, Early Julien, Gladstone, Golden Knob, Queen Caroline, Schoolmaster, Sussex Forge, Yellow Ingestrie, Yorkshire Beauty.

Bush or Pyramid Apples.

Cellini.—K. and T. Sept. to Oct. Medium to large, conical, highly flushed and streaked, and very handsome. Tree forming a natural pyramid, and very early bearer.

It should not, however, be planted on cold, clay soils, where it is subject to canker.

Cox's Orange Pippin.—See also Standards.

Duchess of Oldenburg.—See also Standards.

Ecklinville.—See also Standards.

Frogmore Prolific.—K. and T. Oct. Large, handsome apple, pale yellow, streaked with red, of first-rate quality, a free bearer and strong grower.

Hawthornden (New).—K. Nov. to Dec. Very large, pale green, flushed, and sometimes highly coloured on cheek. Tree, a vigorous grower and heavy cropper. A great improvement on the old Hawthornden.

Keswick Codlin.—K. Aug. to Sept. Medium, conical, pale yellow, somewhat angular in shape; a well-known variety, being a prolific bearer and a good one to give a return quickly.

King of Pippins.—See Standards.

Lord Derby.—K. Nov. Very large, oblong, greenish yellow. Tree, a strong grower and free bearer, the only fault of the fruit for market being its green colour. It rarely fails to produce a good crop. One Kent grower this season had a crop of this variety alone of 2,000 bushels.

Lord Grosvenor.—K. Sept. Large, conical, pale yellow, slightly ribbed. An immense bearer that does remarkably well on heavy soils. A good substitute for Lord Suffield where that variety will not thrive, but not equal to it in quality.

Lord Suffield.—K. Aug. to Sept. Large, conical, pale yellow, very even surface, and of first-rate quality. Where it will succeed it cannot be surpassed, being an early and continuous bearer; but it should not be planted on heavy or shallow soils, or the results will be most unsatisfactory.

The best soil for it is a light, warm loam, with porous subsoil, and even then it will not always succeed.

POTT'S SEEDLING.—See Standards.

PRINCE ALBERT (LANE'S).—K. Oct. to Jan. Large, handsome fruit, pale green, streaked bright red; a very firm apple. It has only come to the front rank during the last few years, having been much too long kept in obscurity. One of the very best to grow for profit, being a fitting companion to Stirling Castle, which variety it succeeds.

STIRLING CASTLE.—K. Sept. Large, round, and somewhat flat, good quality, and immense and certain bearer. One of the very best apples to give a return quickly, and one that does well on almost all soils.

WORCESTER PEARMAIN.—See Standards.

Supplementary List.

The above may be supplemented by the following varieties, many of which are scarcely second to the foregoing, and indeed two or three of the newer varieties below enumerated are likely to prove more valuable than some of the foregoing.

Alfriston, Baumann's Red Winter Reinette, Bismarck, Col. Vaughan, Golden Spire, Loddington, Lady Sudeley, Mank's Codlin, Northern Dumpling, Peasgood's Nonsuch, Professor, Ross Nonpareil, The Queen, Yorkshire Beauty.

Standard Pears.

BEURRE BOSC, OR CALEBASSE.—Oct. to Nov. Large, pyriform; skin, pale brown. A very rich melting pear, grown largely for market.

BEURRE CAPIAUMONT.—Oct. Medium, pyriform, fair quality, and prolific bearing; very hardy.

D

Beurre Diel.—Oct. to Nov. Large, roundish pear. Tree, somewhat spreading, hardy and prolific.

Beurre Hardy.—Oct. Medium size, reddish-brown colour, obovate, rich and juicy. Tree, most vigorous grower. A variety that should be grown by every one.

Clapp's Favourite.—Aug. to Sept. Large, pyriform, highly coloured, and very handsome; quality good. Tree, of good, upright habit, and a vigorous grower. One of the best for exhibition or market.

Conseiller de la Cœur.—Oct. to Nov. Large, pyriform, rich, tender, melting pear. Tree, a most vigorous grower, and deserves much wider cultivation.

Glou Morceau.—Dec. to Jan. Medium size. Flesh, white, tender, and very juicy. Tree, a moderate grower, of a somewhat spreading habit.

Jersey Gratioli.—Sept. to Oct. Medium size, round, rich and sugary. One of the best early autumn pears.

Louise Bonne de Jersey.—Oct. Large, pyriform. A very handsome pear, of first quality. Tree, a moderate grower; habit, upright; free bearer, and a good pear for market.

Marie Louise.—Oct. to Nov. Large, pyriform. Flesh white and buttery, and when well grown, the finest flavoured pear we have, but it should be planted only in good soils as a standard, the tree being tender.

Stewing Pears.—Catillac, and Uvedale's St. Germain.

Bush Pears.

Clapp's Favourite.—See Standards.

Doyenne Boussoch.—Sept. Medium to large, round and very handsome, melting and juicy, quality fair. A most prolific bearer.

Doyenne du Comice.—Nov. Very large, rich and most

delicious flavour. There is no pear to equal it for size and quality combined. The tree is of an upright habit, and moderate bearer.

DUCHESSE D'ANGOULÊME.—Nov. Very large, roundish, obovate, half melting, but rather coarse. Well known as "Duchess" in the market, and largely imported from the Channel Islands and France. Upright habit.

JERSEY GRATIOLI.—See Standards.

LOUISE BONNE DE JERSEY.—See Standards.

PITMASTON DUCHESSE.—Oct. to Nov. Very large, pyriform, handsome; flesh, tender and melting. One of the best to grow for profit, as it commands a ready sale on account of its large size and good appearance.

PRINCESS (RIVERS'S).—Nov. Large, pyriform, melting and juicy. A seedling from Louise Bonne de Jersey, but a more vigorous grower than its parent, and certainly an acquisition. Of upright habit.

CONSEILLER DE LA CŒUR.—See Standards.

MARIE LOUISE D'UCCLE.—Oct. Medium to large, obtuse, pyriform; flesh fine, melting, and richly flavoured. Tree forms a natural pyramid or bush, and is a free bearer, and very hardy.

BEURRE ALEXANDER LUCAS.—Nov. Large, obtuse, pyriform, very handsome pear, but comparatively unknown. Tree, a moderate grower and good bearer; fine showy fruit.

BEURRE CLAIRGEAU.—Nov. Large, pyriform, highly coloured, and very handsome. Fruit of moderate quality. The tree is a strong grower, of good habit, and is a very constant bearer.

DURANDEAU.—Nov. Large, juicy, sweet, and excellent quality. Very handsome in appearance, somewhat like Beurre Clairgeau, but of better quality. Tree, a moderate grower, of an upright habit.

Glou Morceau.—See Standards.

Hessel or Hazel.—Oct. Medium, round, juicy and sweet, but not of high quality. An abundant bearer, and probably at one time more largely grown for market than any other kind.

Williams' Bon Chrétien.—Aug. to Sept. Large, obtuse. Flesh white and melting, with a fine aroma. Tree, a strong grower, with an upright habit. A well-known pear.

The above varieties are all suitable for bush and pyramid forms of culture, and the following additions may also be made:—

Souvenir du Congrès, Beurre Superfin, Brockworth Park, Fondante d'Automne, Madame Treyve, Thompson's, Zépherin Grégoire, Marie Benoist, Gansel's Bergamot, Beurre Bachelier.

Stewing Pears.—Catillac, and Uvedale's St. Germain.

Plums for Standards.

Cox's Emperor.—K. & T. Sept. Large, round, dark red plum. An abundant bearer. Tree, a vigorous grower.

Czar.—K. July and Aug. Large, purple, rich and good. Enormous bearer. Tree, upright in habit, and strong grower. Superior to the Early Prolific, being of larger size.

Gisborne's.—K. Sept. A medium oval, yellow plum of second quality, but being an immense and regular bearer is a profitable one for market growth.

Early Orleans.—K. Aug. Large, round, purplish red, of good quality, largely grown for market, but is being somewhat superseded by Early Prolific and Czar, but being very hardy, it should be by no means omitted.

Old Orleans.—K. Aug. Medium, round, purple plum. A heavy bearer and very hardy.

Pond's Seedling.—K. Sept. An exceedingly large, red, oval plum; highly recommended on account of its large size. Tree, a strong grower of upright habit

Prince Englebert.—K. & T. Sept. A large oval, deep purple fruit, a rich and excellent plum. An enormous bearer, and good for preserving.

Sultan.—K. & T. Aug. A large, round, deep red plum; one that ought to be better known.

Victoria.—K. & T. Sept. A large oval, red plum, sweet and juicy. An enormous cropper, and one that may be termed everybody's plum.

Bush Plums.

Early Prolific.—K. July. Medium, round, purple; an enormous bearer. Tree of moderate growth, and one of the very best for market purposes.

Czar.—See Standards.

Kirke's Blue.—T. Sept. Large, roundish oval, rich and juicy. Tree, a moderate grower, forming good pyramid or bush. Altogether a desirable plum.

Green Gage.—T. Aug. Medium, round, and very rich in flavour. There is no plum to equal it in the richness of its flavour. The tree is a strong grower of good habit.

Early Orleans.—See Standards.

Pond's Seedling.—See Standards.

Prince Englebert.—See Standards.

Cherries for Standards.

Bedford Prolific.—July. A large, black cherry. Tree very hardy.

FROGMORE BIGARREAU.—Mid June. Large, yellowish red, rich and tender. A great bearer.

BIGARREAU NAPOLEON.—July to Aug. Large and fine cherry, red, rich and tender. An abundant bearer.

BIGARREAU KENTISH.—End of July. A large and fine cherry, yellowish red. A regular cropper.

BLACK HEART.—Mid July. A good useful old variety.

GOVERNOR WOOD.—Beginning July. Fine large cherry, light red, flesh tender. Tree, a most vigorous grower.

Cherries for Bush Culture.

ARCHDUKE.—July. Dark red, rich and good. In appearance somewhat like May Duke, but later.

EMPRESS EUGENIE.—End of June. Large, red, early, rich variety of the May Duke. Tree forms a good pyramid.

MAY DUKE.—July. Large, red, rich, and excellent. A well-known old variety, forming a handsome pyramid.

MORELLO.—Aug. to Sept. Dark red, black when ripe, large in size. Very largely grown for market, and a most profitable variety to grow in this form, bearing profusely as a pyramid.

KENTISH.—July. Medium, red; a well-known sort, largely grown in Kent for preserve.

Bush Fruits.

GOOSEBERRIES.

LANCASHIRE LAD.—Large, bright red. A good bearer largely grown, and gathered green to thin the berries. Of a good, upright habit.

CROWN BOB.—Large, red, and a good quality. An abundant bearer, and moderate grower.

WARRINGTON.—Medium red. An extraordinary bearer,

and first class for preserving. More largely grown at one time than any other variety. Pendulous in habit.

WHITESMITH.—A large and fine bush; the best of the whites to grow in quantity.

WHINHAM'S INDUSTRY.—Medium, dull red. Immense bearer, of recent introduction; having a thick skin, it will bear carriage remarkably well when ripe. This variety is also largely picked green, to thin the fruit.

BLACK CURRANTS.

LEE'S PROLIFIC.—A large and fine currant, remarkably rich and sweet. The best for market cultivation. Carter's Champion is sometimes claimed to supersede it, but is certainly no improvement.

BLACK NAPLES.—Large, and of good quality. At one time largely grown, but now superseded by Lee's Prolific.

RED AND WHITE CURRANTS.

LA VERSAILLES.—Red; very large fruit, and enormous sized bunches. When well grown the berries are nearly as large as a cherry, much superior in every way to the Dutch and Grape varieties. Tree, a moderate grower.

HAUGHTON CASTLE.—Red; large size bunches, a very strong grower and moderate bearer.

WHITE GRAPE.—Large; of first quality, good size bunches.

WHITE DUTCH.—Large and fine currant; berries of a good size, and forms a good bush.

RASPBERRIES.

CARTER'S PROLIFIC.—Large and fine, of a dull red colour. An enormous bearer, and altogether the most profitable variety to grow.

FASTOLFF.—Medium; bright red, and good quality Strong, sturdy grower.

CHAPTER V.

PLANTING.

If the plantation is a mixed one, consisting of both top and bottom fruits, it is best to plant the standards first. The most convenient direction for the rows should be chosen, and, if possible, these should run north and south, in order to give the bush trees as much sun as possible. Peg out the position of each tree in order to insure placing the whole in straight lines and at true angles. Having pegged out the first row, next determine the angle, which can be done best by a quarter-staff. Then proceed to peg out the other rows. If this is carefully done, the trees will then appear in straight lines from whatever direction they are viewed. In setting out the ground, it is now needful to bear in mind what roadways may be necessary, in order to afford easy access to all parts of the plantation, for the purposes of cultivating and manuring the ground, and gathering and collecting the fruit. The distance apart at which to plant the standards will be regulated by the bottom fruit intended to be grown, and the nature of the same, etc., as indicated below.

Standard apples, pears, and plums, on good ground, for pyramid or bush forms of the same trees below, may be planted twenty-four feet apart; but where the land is not so good, or currants or gooseberries are intended to be grown beneath, they may be planted eighteen feet apart.

Cherries on good ground thirty feet, or on second quality ground at twenty-four feet.

Between the standards at twenty-four feet apart, the bush trees, if on the paradise or quince stock, may be planted at six feet apart, which would give three trees between each standard, and three rows of bush between each row of standards (Fig. 4). At this distance they

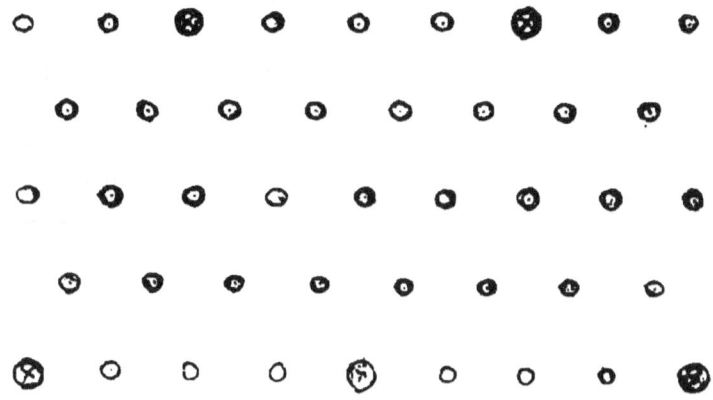

Fig. 4.—⊕ Standard Apples, 24 feet apart.
    o Bush Apples on Paradise Stock, 6 feet apart.

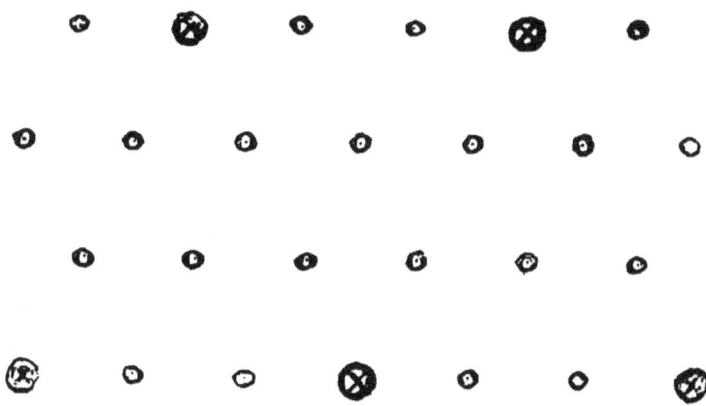

Fig. 5.—⊕ Standard Trees, 24 feet apart.
    o Bush Trees, 8 feet apart.

would yield a quicker and better return for the first six or eight years, but after that they usually become somewhat crowded, and each alternate tree may be removed to form a new plantation. Therefore a better distance for a permanent plantation is to plant the bush trees at eight feet apart, giving two trees between each standard, and two rows between each row of standards (Fig. 5). And, in the same way, if standards are planted at eighteen feet, one pyramid may be planted between each, and one row between each row of standards, or gooseberries may also be planted in the same way at six feet apart. But for gooseberry or currant culture between the standards,

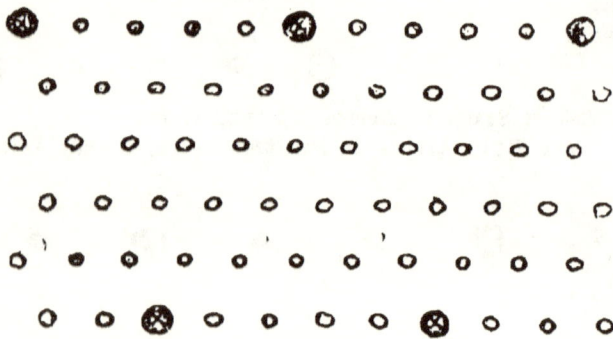

Fig. 6.—⊕ Standard Trees, 25 feet.
o Bushes, 5 feet apart.

the usual distance for ordinary ground is to plant the standards twenty-five feet apart, and the bushes between at five feet apart (Fig. 6). Or, if the land be very rich, the standards may be planted twenty-four feet, and the bushes six feet.

Still another and an excellent arrangement is to plant standard apples or pears twenty-four feet apart, with a pyramid plum between each, and a row of pyramids between each row of standards. Then, between each of these, successively plant a bush fruit, of either gooseberry or black currant, as per Fig. 7.

In planting the standards, it is well to bear in mind the habit of the varieties planted, and to arrange the rows alternately with one tall variety, and the next of a lower

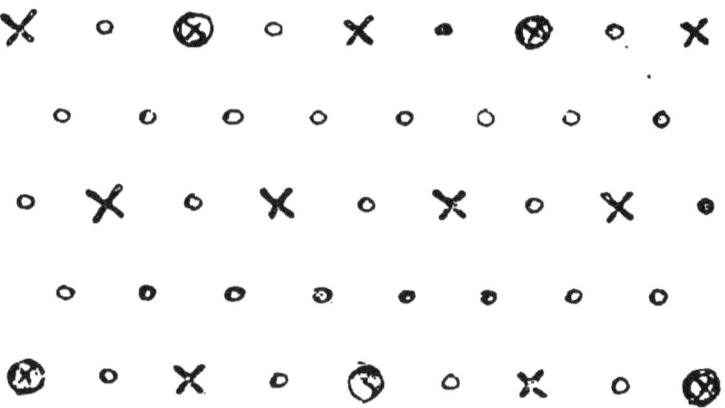

FIG. 7.-- ⊕ STANDARD APPLE.
× PYRAMID PLUM.
o GOOSEBERRY OR CURRANT.

spreading habit. To assist planters in this respect the following table gives the habit of each of the trees mentioned.

HABIT OF TREES.

STANDARD APPLES, SPREADING.

Duchess of Oldenburg, Golden Noble, Warner's King, Cox's Orange, Blenheim Orange, Winter Queening, Wellington, Early Julien, Yorkshire Beauty, Bramley's Seedling, Claygate Pearmain, Gladstone, Queen Caroline.

STANDARD APPLES, UPRIGHT.

Worcester Pearmain, Ecklinville, King Pippin, Norfolk Beefing, Pott's Seedling, Golden Knob, Mannington, Beauty of Kent.

STANDARD PEARS, SPREADING.

Beurre Bosc, Beurre Diel, Glou Morceau, Marie Louise, Hessel or Hazel, Conseiller de la Cœur.

STANDARD PEARS, UPRIGHT.

Beurre Capianmont, Beurre Hardy, Louise Bonne de Jersey, Williams' Bon Chrétien, Clapp's Favourite, Jersey Gratioli.

STANDARD PLUMS, SPREADING.

Cox's Emperor, Early Orleans, Old Orleans, Victoria, Sultan.

STANDARD PLUMS, UPRIGHT.

Czar, Gisborne's, Prince Engelbert, Pond's Seedling.

It is also a great convenience in after years to have each row a distinct variety, and of course as many rows of one variety in succession as you please, but do not break the row by planting two or three sorts.

Now for the actual operation of planting. The land having been previously prepared, as before directed, it will only be needful to dig out a very shallow hole for the tree. But dig it wide enough to admit of all the roots being laid out at full length. If the land, however, requires the application of manure at the time of planting, the hole should be dug slightly deeper, and a small quantity of manure placed in the bottom, with a sprinkling of soil to cover it.

The next operation should be to drive the stakes firmly into their positions, in the centre of each hole. The usual plan is to plant the tree first and stake afterwards, but there are several advantages in placing the stakes first. You avoid the danger of damaging the roots in

PLANTING.

thrusting the stake through, and also the risk of damaging the branches in driving it home. It is also ready for securing the tree immediately on planting, and one other advantage, which is not the least, is that it enables you to arrange the rows in perfectly straight lines at leisure, and permits you to proceed rapidly with the planting when the trees are lifted, thus avoiding the unnecessary exposure of the roots. If full standards are to be planted, the stakes should be seven feet long, allowing eighteen inches to enter the ground, which, if it has been properly prepared, will be loose to that depth. They should be stout, and of some wood that will stand for three years. If only small stakes are used they soon decay; at the end of the first season many will want renewing, and they will require constant attention and renewal for several years. It is therefore by far the most economical plan to provide stout stakes in the first place.

The trees should then be laid out to the holes ready for planting, and each tree should be carefully examined as to its roots. In lifting from the nursery, all the larger roots will be found to be more or less bruised by the cutting of the spade. All these should be trimmed by a clean cut with a sharp knife, and any long, coarse roots should be shortened back. This clean cutting of the roots enables them to quickly form new fibrous roots, and these rapidly establish themselves in the soil.

There is a right way and a wrong in performing even this simple operation. Never hold the tree in such a way that you cut the larger roots with an outside or vertical cut, but cut on the under-side from the centre of the tree towards the outside. The cut portion is then underneath the tree, and lies flatly and firmly on the soil, enabling the newly forming fibres to take a rapid hold of the ground and radiate over it.

Then one operator should hold up the tree, placing it to the south-west side of the stake towards the prevailing wind, whilst the other places on the roots some soil, the finer the better. See that the roots are well spread out, and none of them curled back or doubled under the tree. When covered with fine soil, slightly shake the tree up and down, to help the soil to settle between the fibres, but do not lift enough to draw the roots out; and here it will be found very useful to have a small stake with a round end in one hand, to help to fill in the soil firmly about

Fig. 8. Correct Planting.

the roots, which is better and more safely done at this stage with the stake than with the foot. Then add more soil, and tread it in, taking great care not to bruise the stem or any of the roots. Next add a little more manure, and finish by placing the remainder of the soil on the surface, covering up the tree to the collar, or to the depth at which it has stood in the nursery. Then gently tread the whole, leaving it in a mound. Bear in mind that the object is to place the roots in such a position that they may extend horizontally, spreading in all directions in the surface soil, as shown on Fig. 8, and on no account plant too deeply, causing the roots to ascend in growth towards the surface or to perish in the subsoil (Fig. 9).

Immediately after planting, secure the tree to the stake. Be careful to wrap round the tree a band of straw or hay, or a piece of bagging, and tie the stake firmly to it with strong tar string, making the last tie across the strings between the stake and the tree, thus tightening the whole and securing them against the danger of chafing. These ties will require to be periodically examined, in order to loosen and re-tie any that may require to be so treated. It is essential that the tree should be secured firmly

Fig. 9. Wrong Planting.

against rocking with the wind, as nothing is more hurtful to the young rootlets than to be torn from their hold of the soil by constant motion of the tree; and the difference in growth during the first two or three years between a firmly staked and a wind-rocked tree is marvellous.

Some planters use two stakes, but this is not really necessary, provided the one used is sufficiently strong, and the tree well secured as described.

When the standards are properly planted and secured, the planting of the bush or pyramid trees between them is a very simple and straightforward matter. The lines being already determined, it is only needful with a rod to mark the spaces between, to dig holes and plant the trees in a similar way to that described for the standards. No staking in the case of these bush trees will be necessary.

Raspberries are in some cases planted below apple trees, in which case they should be set out at a distance of four to five feet from row to row, and twelve to fifteen inches from plant to plant in each row. But these are more usually grown in open fields, in which case they are sometimes planted by placing the sets along the open furrow during the time of ploughing, allowing the next furrow to cover the roots. This, however, is a somewhat rough and ready way of doing it, and not one that can be recommended, as the plants are frequently driven somewhat out of their places by the plough, and it is difficult to make good, even work in this way. A far better plan is to plough the whole of the land first, and dig holes for each plant in the ordinary way afterwards. Small holes only are required, and the line of the furrow may generally be taken as a line for each row.

Rabbits.—One matter will, after planting, require some care and watchfulness; namely, the danger of injury to the trees by rabbits. If there should be any in the vicinity of the plantation, it is well to be prepared in time; and if the plantation is a mixed one, and the ground entirely occupied by the trees, it would be the cheapest plan to place wire netting round the whole of the outside. But where standard orchard trees alone are planted, there are other means adopted which are less costly, and answer the purpose fairly well. There are some preparations advertised for painting the stems of the trees to prevent the rabbits from touching them; but these preparations should be used with care, for fear of damage being done to the bark of the trees. Any greasy or sticky preparation covering the bark for a lengthened period is in danger of damaging it. Where furze bushes or trimmings from hedges can be easily obtained, a simple plan is to tie a few of these around the stem of each tree; or three or four laths or loose pieces of bark, which can be obtained from most sawyards, will also answer the purpose.

Labelling.—Another matter which will require immediate attention after planting, is that of securing the names of the varieties planted. It is always well in the first place to take a plan of the plantation, noting each row with the varieties planted in the same. This plan should be carefully preserved in case of any accident to or loss of the labels in the orchard. Various plans are adopted for the labelling of the trees, some using a number stamped upon tin or lead, with a book of reference; but this means is not always satisfactory, and it is often the cause of delay and annoyance to have to procure the book, which is often not at hand when wanted. It is much more convenient, economical, and interesting to have each variety distinctly named in full, the best label for this purpose being Pinches' Patent, which is a cast-iron label with the names in raised characters, plain and indelible, as shown in Fig. 10. This should be attached to a branch of the tree by either galvanized or lead wire, care being taken to leave a sufficiently large loop to allow for the growth of the tree; and even then it is needful to examine the fastenings periodically, and see that no damage is done.

Fig. 10.
Fruit Label.

Shelter.—If the plantation is at all exposed, it is highly important to provide some suitable shelter. Wind-swept plantations suffer exceedingly, especially when young and open between the trees. Shelter may be given most quickly by lines of Lombardy poplar, planted about two feet apart. Its close upright growth affords a good wind break, but it is somewhat objectionable on account of its tendency to draw nourishment from the plants near it. Therefore, if possible, arrange for a roadway between a poplar hedge and the plantation, and if the roots are found to extend across the roadway into the plantation, they should be periodically cut by digging a trench and cutting all roots that cross. A belt of fir trees affords valuable shelter at the outsides, if the position is very exposed, and in some places damsons are used for this purpose, and where they are likely to afford sufficient protection they are the most profitable, as they produce a paying crop. The cluster damson is the best for this purpose, and the trees may be allowed to extend themselves, with very little pruning, until they form a close hedge. Standards of these may be planted at ten feet apart, or, if there is no hedge below, it is best to plant standards at twelve feet apart, and a feathered tree between each.

Strawberries.

Strawberries require such totally different treatment from fruit trees, they are here dealt with separately, as to planting and management. The best soil for them is a strong loam with a cool subsoil, but they will flourish in a great variety of soils. Do not, however, plant them on dry sand, chalk, or dry gravel. In some instances, however, they flourish well on gravel which has in it a mixture of clay.

They are usually grown on large open fields, and grown alone. The soil should be prepared, as for other fruit, by extra deep cultivation, but it is not necessary to trench the land by hand. It can always be done for strawberries in the open fields by horse labour or steam cultivation. Above all, let the land be thoroughly clean, and in good condition, and it should have a heavy coat of manure before planting, as much as forty to fifty tons per acre. This should be applied, if possible, several weeks beforehand, and thoroughly mixed with the soil.

The time of planting is either August or March. The latter is preferable, unless the planting can be done early in the autumn to allow the plants to establish themselves in the soil, otherwise they are liable to be lifted by winter frosts. To escape this danger many growers prefer to plant in March. The land should be levelled and rolled before commencing to plant, and marked out in lines thirty inches apart, and fifteen to twenty inches in the row. In Kent, where large quantities are planted, a marker is used, made in the form of a light wheel, having pegs at the distance apart that the plants are to stand in the row, and this being pushed along the row marks the distances quickly and evenly. The runners for planting are usually selected from strong two-year-old plants, and they are dibbled in with a setting stick, care being taken to press the plant firmly to the soil, and not to bury the crown.

In a short time the young plants throw out strong runners, which are usually cut off during the first summer, and to do this they require going over three or four times at least. The land must be kept clean both by horse and hand hoeing, and in autumn a mould-board plough is used to throw a furrow each way between the rows, casting it towards the plants to protect them and assist drainage. These furrows are levelled in the following spring by the horse hoe, and the ground is kept clean until the plants are in bloom. Barley or oat straw is then spread between the plants to keep the fruit clean. The straw can be removed after the fruit is picked, and either stacked away for future use, or carted to the yards. A good crop is usually taken the second season after planting. After the fruit has been picked, the straw is raked off and the foliage trimmed, and by the second year the land will require a good dressing of stable manure applied in autumn. Also soot and artificial manures may be applied advantageously each year. The duration of the crop is usually five to six years, after which the yield declines, and the plant is not worth retaining.

Varieties of Strawberries

SIR JOSEPH PAXTON.—This is at the present time more largely grown than any other variety, being a heavy cropper, rich in flavour, and what is highly important to the market grower, stands packing well. Consequently it is more largely used than any other for punnetting.

VISCOMTESSE HERICART DE THURY.—Fine large fruit, which stands well the wet weather, its abundant foliage protecting the flowers and fruit. Fine for preserving.

SIR CHARLES NAPIER.—A fine late variety, large and good cropper, and travels well.

ELTON PINE.—A showy fruit, and highly coloured right through the flesh. On this account it is much prized for preserving.

ELEANOR.—One of the latest, and on that account useful; free grower, and hardy.

LAXTON'S NOBLE.—This variety, though of recent introduction, has come rapidly to the front as a market variety. It is the earliest out of doors, ripening ten days or a fortnight earlier than Sir J. Paxton. This is a great consideration, enabling the grower to realize good prices, and it also helps to prolong the season, and to distribute the work of gathering and marketing more evenly. It is borne in bunches, and the fruit is very large, round in shape, and of a high colour. On some light soils it is considered of somewhat poor flavour and the flesh light and woolly, but on heavy soil the flesh is firm and the flavour really good. The plant being a vigorous grower and a heavy cropper makes it altogether a most profitable variety to grow.

AFTER CULTIVATION OF ORCHARDS AND PLANTATIONS.

For *orchard* or *standard trees*, if on grass, not much ground cultivation can be given. It is not a good plan to take crops of hay from an orchard. Long grass during its growth so shades the ground, and excludes sun and air, that it is very hurtful to the trees, and causes the young fibrous roots to decay. It is a far better plan to pasture such land with sheep, especially if they are fed at the time with corn or cake. The land then becomes enriched instead of impoverished, and a good supply of nutriment to the trees is maintained. Otherwise it is needful to apply manure on the surface periodically, in order to encourage the formation and growth of the fibrous roots near the surface.

Further directions as to the fit treatment and improvement of fruit trees on grass land will be found in the chapter upon renovating old orchards.

If the standard trees, however, are planted on arable land, it is preferable to keep it open, and not to lay it down to grass for the first few years, but if possible keep it cultivated, manured, and cropped with any green crops, but not with corn. Such cultivation may be done by horses, if great care is taken not to rub or damage the trees, and also not to plough too deeply near to them. If the trees are set out evenly, and in true lines in all directions, most of the ground may be covered by such horse cultivation, by crossing in two or three directions, but there will always be some ground near to the tree not moved. This must be treated by hand. It will require hoeing in summer to keep clear of the weeds, and should be forked over in the winter, or dug lightly with the spade.

Mixed Plantations.

The cultivation here will much depend upon what is planted, and how closely. If bush apples, pears or plums are planted, with no strawberries between, it will be possible to use the hoe or scarifier for the first year or two, but it is hardly possible to use the plough to advantage in such plantations. If the intervening land between the trees be filled up with strawberries or other more permanent ground crop, hand cultivation entirely will have to be resorted to. In any case the work will have to be done principally by hand. This weeding, forking, and digging of the plantations is usually performed by piece work, the prices of which are given in Chap. VII. Manure is applied according to the nature of the soil, the crop, and the growth of the trees. It is well to arrange this, if possible, in rotation; taking, for instance, the third of a plantation each year.

CHAPTER VI.

PRUNING.

On this question there is considerable diversity of opinion, and rightly so, for it admits of it. The conditions under which the pruning is performed are so different that the same practice under varying conditions leads to widely different results. Therefore, study first all the circumstances affecting the case, then proceed accordingly.

I will now endeavour to indicate some of the points to be studied, with directions for treatment in particular cases.

Standard and Half Standard Apples at the time of Planting.—Supposing you have obtained trees which have been properly treated in the nursery, you will have a head varying in size according to the age of the tree. The considerations that would govern you as to the amount of pruning to be given at planting would be these: the time of planting, the condition and quality of the ground, the age and the formation of the tree, and to some extent the variety. If the tree is young, with a head of only young growth, you may generally shorten back pretty hard, especially if planted in autumn in ground that is rich, and in good condition. In such a case you may cut back at least two-thirds of the growth, and always cut clean away any surplus number of branches. The effect of this pruning under the above conditions will be the production of good strong growth, and the formation of a strong foundation for the future tree. But supposing the tree to be older, and one that has in the head older wood, upon which there may be already some fruit buds, it is necessary to be much more sparing with the knife, not cutting back more than half of the young growth of the leading shoots. Should there, however, be too many of these, cut away all surplus ones, in order to keep the centre or foundation of the tree well open. A standard tree of four or five years' growth, that has had proper treatment up to that time, would have already a good foundation with considerable wood in bearing condition. In this case it would be the greatest folly to adopt the old, and still too prevalent, practice of cutting in the growth almost to the main stem, and would be undoing at least the work of two years, and simply losing so much time. The object which should constantly be borne in mind is to obtain the largest tree in the shortest time with the greatest extension of branches.

The old system of continued hard pruning for several years certainly has the effect of producing abundance of strong growth; but it is so much growth in the wrong place and to a wrong purpose. This annual shortening causes the tree to become what is known as mop-headed, with a quantity of rank wood growth closely matted together, half of which has to be entirely cut away. And the again repeated shortening in the absence of fruit buds, which cannot form under such treatment, causes only a fresh outburst of useless side growth.

To Summarize.—If the trees are young, the ground is good, and the planting done in autumn, you may venture to prune tolerably hard; but if the trees are older, or the ground not so rich, or the planting through any circumstances delayed until the spring, be very sparing of the knife; cut hard the first season only when all the circumstances lead you to expect a response to the knife in good strong growth. Otherwise wait until the following season, when the tree will have established itself firmly in the soil, by getting a good root hold, and will then be in a better position to answer to the knife. It is frequently seen that when trees are planted under any adverse circumstances, and pruned close at the time of planting, and especially when a dry season ensues, such trees present the appearance of mere stakes, and the root action will be much slower and much less through the restriction at the top. It is better to err on the safe side; which is, I firmly believe, to wait until the tree has taken hold of the soil and commenced its root action.

Having so pruned the tree in the first place, as to form a good foundation and a well-balanced head, the after treatment required is very simple. Remove completely all surplus branches. Keep the head well opened to admit all the sun and air possible to ripen and perfect the fruit, and also the very important, but much overlooked, point, to allow of the proper ripening and maturing of the wood and of the fruit buds. Remove any surplus side growth, thereby encouraging the formation of fruit spurs upon all the leading branches. In shortening the main branches, always cut close behind an underneath or outward pointing bud, and not to the top or inward one.

Standard pears and plums require very much the same treatment as that described for apples. Cherries, however, should have the knife used very much more sparingly, and after the first year or two require no shortening and very little thinning. There is great danger of gumming by the free use of the knife; and, if the branches are allowed to extend, they are soon covered with fruit spurs, which, producing abundant crops, check and regulate the superabundant wood.

Bush Apples.—In pruning this class of tree, a great deal will depend upon the variety, some growing so much stronger than others. In the first place, taking a variety that makes but little growth, all the pruning that is necessary when the tree is procured, supposing it to be two or three years old, and the number of shoots from four to eight, will be as follows. The main object will be to open the centre of the tree. This is done by simply cutting the shoots that may be crossing each other to within two or three eyes of the base of the shoot. The leading branches may then be cut back about two-thirds of their length to an outer bud. This may be repeated each succeeding year, bearing in mind the form of the tree desired. The result of the pruning will have been to stimulate wood growth and the formation of fruit spurs. A tree with the centre well opened, fully exposed to the sun and air, is capable of producing large and fine flavoured fruit.

With regard to the stronger growing varieties, the pruning will be much the same, only that the leading shoots will not require to be cut back so closely as the weaker growing kinds; they must be allowed more freedom of growth, which will result in the development of fruit spurs instead of rampant wood growth, and when once in fruit they will check themselves naturally. When the trees have reached the height of from four to six feet the leading shoots may be cut back more closely, with the view of keeping the tree down, and not so much exposed to the wind, or well below the standard trees above them. In many fruit gardens along the south coast, and in other exposed situations, the trees are trained as open bushes, and allowed to reach the height of six to eight feet, when they are pruned to an even height, forming flat tops of a uniform height. This affords the greatest possible protection to the individual plants, as the storms sweep over the level tops with comparatively little harm.

Bush Pears.—This form of tree is usually being worked on the quince stock, and requires very little pruning when once the bush is well formed, and this stock should always be used for this form of tree, unless the soil be very light and dry. The trees are usually planted at from two to four years old, having from four to eight branches, about two or three feet in length. The first pruning should be to cut back these shoots to about one foot from the base, with the result that each will throw out two or three good leading growths. The subsequent pruning would be to shorten the leading shoots, and leave a few smaller branches as the tree extends, always keeping the centre of the tree open and clear from surplus growth.

Gooseberries.—These require rather hard pruning for the first year or two. Thin out any surplus shoots, and shorten the remainder by at least half their length. In cutting, they require exactly contrary treatment to that of the standard trees in this respect. Cut behind the upright bud, the object here being to lead the branches as upright as possible, and to keep them from drooping to the ground, this being the general tendency with the most prolific gooseberries, the weight of the fruit soon bringing the branches down. Subsequently allow the main branches to extend, but keep them a good distance apart. Shorten all side growth to within two or three eyes of the main branch, to encourage the formation of spurs; but as the main branches extend, allow some side growths to remain and also extend, where space will allow. Always keep the tree sufficiently open to permit the hand to pass freely to the centre for gathering and pruning purposes. Gooseberries fruit not only on the spurs, but also upon well-ripened wood of last year's growth. By keeping the trees well opened it allows them to fruit on the inside as well as at the extremities. Summer pinching may be adopted to advantage, as it assists in ripening fruit, and also in the formation and maturing of fruit spurs. Do not allow gooseberries to fruit much for the first season or two, and what fruit there is should be gathered green, which does not so much exhaust the tree.

Currants.—These may be treated much in the same way as described for the gooseberry, only keep the tree more open, with greater spaces between the branches. Strong fruiting spurs are formed upon old wood, producing, upon thinly dispersed branches, large bunches of fruit thickly set in clusters, so thick indeed that they hang in perfect masses from the branches. The fruit is also developed fully, and is much more easily and quickly gathered than when allowed to be more thinly dispersed upon crowded trees. Summer pruning of red currants is most useful. Shorten all useless side growths in June. Then all that is required in the winter pruning is to cut back the remainder of the summer pinching, to within one or two eyes of the branch, and to shorten the growth of the leading branches by half or two-thirds. This treatment sounds somewhat severe, but it is the most satisfactory one.

Black Currants.—These require entirely different treatment from the foregoing. Whereas the red currant forms fruiting spurs, the black currant does not, but fruits principally on the young wood. Therefore the growth may be allowed to remain much closer together. Remove all weakly shoots and immature growth, and leave much of the strongest of the current year's growth at full length, the older branches being removed to make room for the young growth, and to keep the tree sufficiently open and properly balanced. They may be allowed to spread low and to extend to large bushes.

Raspberries.—When the canes are planted, they are at once shortened to within about nine inches or a foot of the ground. This will cause them to throw up two or three strong canes the following summer. The after pruning required is the removal of all spent fruiting canes in autumn. Then, during winter or spring, remove any surplus young canes by cutting away close to the ground, and shorten the remainder to about two to four feet from the ground, according to age and strength of stool. In the case of some of the taller varieties, however, it is necessary to leave them longer, in which case they are usually tied together for support; but for open field culture, where they are not staked, it is needful to keep them short, so that they may support the weight of the fruit.

THE BEST TIME TO PRUNE.

There is some difference of opinion as to this point. But theory has to give way to practice, and probabilities to possibilities. To those who have large plantations to deal with, it is not possible to do it all at one time; but the work has to be extended over a considerable period, and to be performed according to labour available, and as other work will allow. It is usually commenced immediately on the fall of the leaf, and continued through the winter months; but where it is possible to get it done in a comparatively short period, there is no doubt that the safest time to do it is after the turn of winter, when the severest weather is past, say about February.

In some seasons, when the weather is favourable to late

growth, which is followed by immature and badly ripened wood, and when the pruning under such circumstances is done in autumn, the severe winter following will damage much of the wood, and cause gaps and vacancies in the trees; whereas, if the pruning is deferred until the spring, any such damaged wood can be removed, and the sound wood selected for retention. Therefore, where pruning has to be commenced in autumn, select the hardiest kinds and the best ripened wood to operate upon first, and such as is also most sheltered. The wood and pith are more liable to damage when the pruning has taken place; but when pruned shortly before the sap rises, the wounds quickly heal.

CHAPTER VII.
COST AND RETURNS PER ACRE.

DISTANCES FOR TREES AND QUANTITIES PER ACRE.

	Distance. Feet.	Number per Acre.
Standard Trees, Apples, Pears, Plums	24	75
With Bush Fruit, Gooseberries or Currants, between Standards	4	2,647
With Bush Apples, Pears, or Plums between	6	1,135
Or Bush Apples, Pears, or Plums, if on richer soil	8	605
Or Standard Trees	21	99
Bush Apples, Pears, or Plums between	7	790
Or Standard Trees	18	134
Bush Apples, Pears, and Plums between	6	1,076
Or Bush Apples, Pears, and Plums between	9	401

DISTANCES, IF EACH GROWN SEPARATELY.

	Distance. Feet.	Number per Acre.
Standard Apples, Pears, or Plums, on poor soil	18	134
Standard Apples, Pears, or Plums, on better soil	21	99
Standard Apples, Pears, or Plums, on rich soil	24	75
Standard Cherries	30	48
Bush or Pyramid Apples, or Pears on Dwarfing stocks	6	1,210
Bush or Pyramid Apples, Pears, or Plums, stronger grown on free stocks and rich soil	9	537
Filberts	12	302
Currants and Gooseberries on poor soils	4	2,722
Currants and Gooseberries on richer soils	5	1,742
Raspberries, 5 ft. rows by	1	8,712
Raspberries, 4 ft. rows by	1	10,890
Strawberries, 2 ft. 6 in. rows by	1½	11,616
„ „ „ „	1	17,424

COST OF TREES AND PLANTS,

This varies considerably, according to age and quality.

Standard Trees of Apples, Pears, Plums, and Cherries, from £5 to £10 per 100.

Half Standard Apples, Pears, Plums, and Cherries, £4 to £7 10s. per 100.

Bush Trees of Apples, Pears, Plums, and Cherries, from £2 10s. to £5 per 100.

Pyramid Apples, Pears, Plums, and Cherries, from £5 to £10 per 100.

Gooseberries, from 10s. to 15s. per 100.
Currants, Black and Red, from 8s. to 12s. per 100.
Raspberries, from 25s. to 35s. per 1,000.
Strawberry Runners, from 6s. to 10s. per 1,000.

COST OF PREPARING LAND.

Steam cultivator, twice over, including coals and water, 30s. to 40s. per acre.

Double ploughing with subsoil plough, 30s. per acre.

Digging, one spade deep, 4d. to 6d. per rod, £2 13s. 4d. to £4 per acre.

Digging, two spades deep, 1s. to 1s. 6d. per rod, £8 to £12 per acre.

COST OF CULTIVATION AND PRUNING.

Digging between trees with spade or fork, 20s. to 30s. per acre.

Hoeing according to weediness, 20s.

Pruning Standard Trees, 20s. per acre.

Pruning Black Currants, 18s. per acre.

Pruning Red Currants, 22s. per acre.

Pruning Gooseberries, 25s. to 30s. per acre.

Pruning Raspberries, 9s. to 12s. per acre.

COST OF PICKING FRUIT, AND YIELD PER ACRE.

For these figures I am indebted to Mr. Cecil Hooper, who has carefully collected the information from many Kent growers

	Rough cost per ton.			Rough cost per acre.	Average yield per acre.	Gross return per acre.
	£	s.	d.	£	Tons.	£
Strawberry	3	18	0	8	2	42
Raspberry	5	0	0	10	2	46
Gooseberry	1	14	0	5	3	25
Red Currant	2	0	0	4	2	30

COST AND RETURNS PER ACRE.

	Rough cost per ton.	Rough cost per acre.	Average yield per acre.	Gross return per acre.
	£ s. d.	£	Tons.	£
Black Currant	4 0 0	8	2	34
Plum Standards	1 0 0	7	7	100
Damson „	2 0 0	12	6	96
Cherry „	2 6 8	9	4	100
Apple „	0 14 0	7	6	60
Pear „	0 11 8	7	5	50

The following facts may also be interesting, as showing the continuous yield of fruit from one apple tree during a term of ten years. I can vouch for their accuracy, as they were furnished by a friend of mine in Essex.

The tree was a Warner's King, of pyramidal form, and was planted at Ramsden, in Essex, in November, 1871.

    1872 Crop, 3 large Apples.
    1873 „ ... ... 1½ pecks.
    1874 „ ... ... 2 „
    1875 „ ... ... 4 „
    1876 „ ... ... 6 „
    1877 „ ... ... 7 „
    1878 „ 2 or 3 Apples.
    1879 „ ... ... 6 „
    1880 „ ... ... 5 „
    1881 „ ... ... 4 „
    1882 „ ... ... 3 „

Thus the average crop for the ten years was four pecks per year. These he sold in Chelmsford market at an average of 1s. 6d. per peck.

The tree occupies a space of not more than 3 square

yards; and calculating an acre of such trees 8 feet apart, or 681 per acre, the gross return would be £204 per acre yearly.

CHAPTER VIII.
RENOVATING OLD ORCHARDS.

Many of the old farm orchards in this country are in a most deplorable condition, the result of utter neglect, lack of knowledge, or want of care, and probably in many cases the three combined. Do not, however, too hastily condemn, cut down, and grub up such orchards, but carefully examine their condition. See whether sufficient life and vigour remain in the trees to pay for an attempt at resuscitation. Remember the time that it takes for fruit trees to grow and develop before arriving at maturity. If the trees are not too old, and the situation is at all promising, and the soil suitable, or capable of improvement, spare the trees. I have seen some wonderful transformations in such orchards after a year or two of careful attention.

First ascertain what varieties the orchard contains. If they are suitable, and worth retaining, by all means keep them. Such trees should during the autumn or winter be carefully treated in the way of pruning and cleaning. Cut away all interlacing branches, and do it with no sparing hand, laying all parts of the tree sufficiently open to admit the sun and air. Entirely remove branches where they are too thick, and clear away all superfluous and twiggy growth, leaving sufficient young growth and blossom buds for future cropping, and especially retain all the fruit buds and spurs which are closely set upon

RENOVATING OLD ORCHARDS.

the leading branches. But a word of caution is here needful as to some varieties, such as Devonshire Quarrenden or Worcester Pearmain, which fruit only on the terminal buds of the current season's growth.

In cutting away branches, where it is needful to use a saw, cut as close as possible to the union, taking great care not to allow the branch, in falling, to split and tear away a portion of the wood or bark. To avoid this, cut round the under side of the branch before sawing through from above. In every case of using the saw, be very careful to trim off all roughness left by the saw with a sharp knife, and finish with a clean cut of the bark round the outside. This should be done in order to allow the wound to heal over as soon as possible by the growth of fresh bark, which it will rapidly do after a clean cut as above directed.

In thinning some of the outer branches which are difficult to reach by hand, it will be needful to use one of the pruning appliances for this purpose, one of the best being the one shown (Fig. 11). But it is always best, where possible, to use the knife; and in the case of all small growth let each shoot be shortened with a clean cut behind the bud. Two useful hand pruners are also shown (Figs. 12 and 13).

Fig. 11.

Fig. 12.   Fig. 13.

In the case of any tree which is known to be of a worthless or inferior variety, if of apples or pears, it deserves consideration whether such trees are sufficiently young and vigorous to be worth re-grafting. If they are fairly healthy, and not too old, considerable time may be gained by re-grafting. To prepare for this operation, select three to six branches of moderate size, shortening them back to within two or three feet of the main stem, cutting clean away any large or crooked branches. The trees may be thus prepared at any time during winter. The grafting must, of course, be done in the spring, when each of the branches left may be grafted with some approved variety.

Crown or rind grafting is the mode usually adopted. The scions should be cut in February, and firmly bedded in the soil. These scions, or future grafts, should be selected from strong, well-ripened wood of the last season's growth; and it is very important that they should be taken from trees that are healthy, and free from canker and other diseases. Some of the diseases, canker particularly, are well known to be hereditary, and if existing in the tree from which the scion was taken, would probably re-appear in the grafted tree after two or three seasons' growth.

The scions having been previously cut and prepared as

above, it is best to leave the actual operation until the flow of sap is fairly brisk. Select the scion and cut into the length, leaving two or three buds above the point of insertion. Then cut the lower half with a sloping splice cut, ending in a wedge-shaped point. A small notch should then be cut in the upper part of the splice to rest on the stock. If the stock has five or six branches of but moderate size, one graft only should be inserted in each, and should be placed upon the upper side. Make one clean upward cut through the bark the length of the splice on the scion, and raise it on one side with the spatula of the knife. Then slip the scion under the bark until the shoulder, as shown in Fig. 14, rests upon the stock, or end of the branch that has been cut off. Then tie firmly round, and cover the union and the end of the stock with clay or grafting wax. The latter is best for standard trees. A good preparation may be bought ready prepared, called L'homme-Lefort grafting wax, which can be obtained of most seedsmen or sundriesmen, or it may be made as follows: One part of suet, two parts of Burgundy pitch, four parts beeswax, and three parts of turpentine. Melt over a gentle fire, and mix together, adding more turpentine if found needful. Apply with a thin lath, taking care to completely exclude the air from the wounds. If only two or three large branches are left on the stock two grafts may be inserted in each.

FIG. 14.—CROWN GRAFTING.

The following are a few strong-growing apples suitable for use in re-grafting :—

Bramley's Seedling, Blenheim Orange, Ecklinville, Golden Noble, Hawthornden (New,) Loddington, Lord Derby, Lord Grosvenor, The Queen, Warner's King, Winter Queening, Tower of Glamis, Alfriston, Frogmore Prolific, Worcester Pearmain, Professor.

Care must be taken to untie the graft before damage is done, as such trees having superabundant sap are apt to swell very rapidly when the graft starts, which graft will require some support for the first year or two to prevent it from blowing out. This can easily be done by tying a small stake to each branch and securing the graft to it. Trees thus treated, if grafted with a good variety, will often bear the second season, and in four years' time make good progress, and I have seen them in some cases bear bushels of fine fruit. It may also be mentioned here, that in some cases where trees are considerably cankered, this plan of re-grafting with a healthy, vigorous variety, will give back new life, health, and vigour to the tree. In the case of plums and cherries, re-grafting will not answer, the severe cutting back causing them to gum.

Another condition in which trees are usually found in old orchards, is one in which they are covered with moss and lichen. The first care of the cultivator should be to remove this. It may be done in the following manner. Obtain fresh lime, which, when it is slaked sufficiently to run into perfect dust, should be applied to the trees as fresh and hot as possible, throwing it amongst the branches upon a moist and damp day. When thus thrown into the trees it will ascend in clouds, and the branches and moss being wet, the dust will adhere to them, and it will soon cause the moss to loosen and fall off. Or the lime may be dissolved in water and applied to the trees with an old garden pump or syringe, which has the same effect. Then scrape off from the stem and the larger branches all the old and loose bark. This may be done by a small hoe or piece of iron hooping. Such loose bark is a receptacle and safe retreat for all kinds of insect pests, and when it is removed the bark should be washed with a mixture of lime, tobacco juice, and quassia; and if thus dressed, it will soon present a clean, bright, and healthy appearance.

As to the improvement of the ground, and the treatment of the roots of such trees, much may be done in this direction. There are some who advocate severely cutting back the roots by digging a trench a few feet from the stems all round the trees, and filling in this trench with fresh soil. The addition of the fresh soil undoubtedly does good by supplying the tree with fresh nutriment; but by cutting back the roots in the way named, I consider that as much harm as good is done by it, and the tree is considerably checked in growth for one or two years. A better plan is to dig the surface round the trees for a space of six or eight feet from the stem, but on no account let this digging be too deeply done. Merely turn over the turf, if there is grass below the trees, to a depth of three or four inches, the object being not to cut away or disturb any of the roots, but to feed, strengthen, and encourage them. The mere opening of the soil, and allowing the sun and air to penetrate, is in itself of some advantage, but it should be followed up by the application of suitable manure on the surface. This will encourage the formation of fresh fibres, which will soon result in a general improvement in the tree throughout. In some cases I have seen this digging carried out far too vigorously and too deeply, thus cutting away a great portion of fibre and smaller rootlets which are the most valuable, and in the best position of all for the production of good fruit. This digging to too great a depth again checks and retards the growth of the tree until it has had time to recover from the effects. Sometimes, in the case of large orchards, the plough is used in breaking up the turf. It answers the purpose in a somewhat rough way, but there is the danger of going too deeply, to the damage of the tree as above described, and in using the plough it is also important to turn over the whole of the ground between the trees. Therefore, some amount of hand labour has to be resorted to as well, and I doubt whether there is much saving by the use of the plough in this case.

Immediately on breaking up the ground, apply a moderate dressing of fresh lime. This will be found beneficial in many ways. It is not only a commodity which is very necessary to the healthy growth of fruit trees, especially of apples, but it helps to decompose the vegetable matter in the freshly turned soil, thus preparing it for the food of the tree, and also to destroy many grubs, larvæ, and other insect pests. Soot may also be applied in the same way with considerable benefit. It is a valuable agent in producing colour in the fruit. If this digging up and dressing with lime is performed in the autumn, it will be well not to apply manure until the spring. This may be done by spreading over the surface a good coating of farmyard or stable manure. But if these are not easily obtainable, recourse may be had to other valuable materials, such as shoddy, furriers' waste clippings, and tanyard refuse. These all contain valuable elements of fertility, and are most of them lasting manures. Other artificial manures may be applied; but in using these, it is needful to study the natural composition of the soil, and also to note what particular ingredients may be absent or deficient, in order that these only may be supplied. See also Chap. II.

The effect of this breaking up of the soil and manuring round the tree is wonderful. You immediately see vigorous healthy growth of wood, and followed by fruit in most cases double or treble the size of that produced by the neglected trees. Whilst the thinning of the wood and opening of the trees, allowing sun and air to penetrate, in addition to the application of lime, soot, phosphate and oxide manures, the ripening and colouring of the fruit will be properly performed; and instead of having a quantity of small, colourless, immature fruit, you will have a greater bulk of good, sound, highly-coloured produce, properly matured, and such as will command a good price in any market.

CHAPTER IX

GATHERING, PACKING, AND DISTRIBUTING.

NEXT in importance to growing the fruit is the matter of gathering and disposing of it. In the first place, as to gathering. There has been in times past, as to farm orchards, little science or care displayed in gathering the fruit. The plan adopted might be picturesque, and might answer the purpose where only small fruit was grown for cider-making, but it is not one that can be adopted where good fruit is produced. The old style of scaling the trees with ladders, and shaking down the fruit, would only do where it was of little value. In the most vigorous shaking given to the trees there were always a few stragglers who survived the shock, and these were dealt with by the use of a long pole. Such a method is only admissible in the case of fruit intended for cider-making.

Time to Gather.

As to the early varieties and those intended to be sent direct to market, it is important to gather them as early as possible, and many of them may be gathered even before they are ripe, as allowance has to be made for the time that must elapse between gathering and the consumption of the fruit, and many of these early varieties ripen very quickly after gathering and last but a very short time in a fit condition for use. Even some of the later or mid-season varieties may be gathered before they are ripe under special circumstances. For instance, if the crop should be somewhat short and prices high early in the season, it will in some cases pay the cultivator to gather some varieties even before they have attained their full size. One of the varieties that will often pay for treating in this way, is the Warner's King. But this matter can only be determined by the condition of the market at the time.

In gathering fruit, especially apples and pears, to be stored for mid-season or late use, it is needful to allow them to remain on the tree until fully matured. A general fault in gathering for storing is perhaps to gather too early. This results in the fruit shrinking in the stores, causing the rind to shrivel and giving the fruit a soft, leathery, and unattractive appearance, besides being of poor quality through not having been properly supplied with the juices and saccharine matter which are formed during the later stages of development, and which are essential to the good keeping and good quality of the fruit.

All soft fruits, such as plums and cherries, must of course be gathered as soon as ready.

The operation of gathering from the tall standard trees requires more care than is usually bestowed upon it. The fruit may be gathered into a bag slung over the shoulder by a cord from corner to corner, leaving the mouth open, but in using such bag great care is needed not to bruise or damage the fruit, and it is far better to use a small handled basket. Such basket may be slung from the ladder by a simple pot-hook, and the fruit will not be so much in danger of being bruised. Avoid placing a ladder against the tree, but use one with a wide base, with a pole hinged to the top for support.

Packing the Fruit.

Apples, pears, and plums are mostly sent to market in baskets known as sieves and half-sieves. The fruit should be at once graded and sorted, each sort being kept distinct. This sorting and grading is an important operation, and is one that is much neglected in this country to the great loss of the grower. It is frequently the case that fruit from farm orchards is gathered and all varieties are mixed together, very little, if any, attention is given to grading, and it is sent to market in this condition, often with early, mid-season, and late varieties, cooking and dessert, large and small, in one mixture. It is not surprising that foreign apples are preferred to English when this is the case. Who can cook such a mixture of fruit as this? Foreign apples, on the other hand, being carefully graded, and only one variety together, the cook knows exactly what she has, and the cooking quality is uniform.

Smaller packages than half-sieves may be adopted with advantage in the case of the choicest dessert kinds. We may learn much from the French in respect to the packing of such fruit. The careful and tasteful way in which they send their fruit to market, and the attractive form in which it is packed and displayed, have a great deal to do with the favour which it finds with consumers; and

FIGS. 15, 16, 17.—CHIP BASKETS.

the adoption of similar modes in this country will be found to pay well. Such specimens of choice fruit as may be selected in gathering, should be packed in small packages. Many such packages of a suitable nature are now made at very reasonable prices.

Soft fruits must be dealt with as they ripen. It will pay to gather all the best quality and pack in small punnets ready for retail purchasers, or in small square card boxes or square chip baskets. These are made to fit into larger packing cases, in which they are forwarded to the agent or salesman. (Fig. 15.) If fruit thus packed is good and even in quality throughout, the buyers soon find it out, and purchase accordingly. One great advantage in thus packing the fruit is, that the small purchasers get the fruit without its being re-packed, and no handling is needful from the time it leaves the garden to its arrival at the consumer's.

After selecting the largest and best in this way, the smaller fruit of raspberries, strawberries, and currants will be almost as good for preserving purposes. These are picked into peck baskets, and raspberries into small tubs. Some large growers, who have a quantity to dispose of, will contract with a jam factory months beforehand, and in some cases for a succession of years even, at fixed prices, the fruit, of course, being gathered and sent in as it becomes ready.

Plums, being also soft fruits, are treated in the same way; but I would strongly urge growers to take much more pains with the choice dessert plums, in the way of packing them in small light baskets or boxes, putting them up in an attractive and tasty manner, so that they may be handed to the consumer without being rubbed and mauled about by the various hands they may pass through.

Pears.—Here again the choice dessert varieties are worthy of much more care in packing than they receive at present. For this small shallow boxes may be used, the fruit being packed closely in single layers, placing a small quantity of soft material at the bottom of the boxes, with a little also between each fruit, wedging each layer tightly together; then fill up with some soft material on the top, so that the lid presses firmly on the fruit. This is important, in order to prevent the fruits from moving and rubbing each other. Boxes of proper dimensions can easily be obtained of packing-case makers at a moderate price. The best and cheapest packing material to use is wood wool, specially made for the purpose. It is light, elastic, and clean, and made of wood which is free from smell.

Apples.—The choicest dessert apples may also be packed in the same way, and for really prime dessert fruit would pay for the cost of packing. It is not necessary to use tissue paper in which to wrap each fruit of apples and pears, as wood wool is so clean that it adheres but very little to the fruit; but at the same time with really good specimens it is desirable to do so. A little labour, with the small cost incurred, is well repaid. Ever bear in mind that dessert fruit should be made to look as clean and attractive as possible. A little taste displayed in the packing of each fruit with white or tinted tissue paper, and the boxes margined with ornamental paper, often ensures a ready sale for foreign fruit of even second-rate quality. The dressing and packing of choice fruit can easily be done at the homestead by women and children, who with a little practice soon do it quickly and well.

As to the more bulky fruit which has to be sent to market in large quantities, such as apples and pears, two things are most essential; namely, to keep the sorts distinct, and grade the fruit to even sizes. This cannot be emphasized too much. A basket of apples or pears with several sorts mixed, though each may be equally valuable by itself, would be of considerably less value in the market than a basket of each variety separate. And never top up the basket with larger selected fruits; for although this is a common practice, it brings its own swift reward. It is immediately detected and, suspicion being aroused, prices rule accordingly. Therefore here, as in all other things, honesty is the best policy. To grade the fruit, empty the baskets out on the tables, or trays made for the purpose, lined with thick felt to prevent bruising. The sorter then, with the fruit in front, draws it forward and passes the various sizes to right and left into the different cases, putting into a separate basket any diseased or inferior fruit.

Distribution.

The mode adopted with regard to the marketing and distribution of fruit must be determined by each grower according to his individual position and circumstances, the quantity and variety of the fruit grown, and the character of and distance from market. The employment of a fruit salesman as an agent in distribution is in many cases needful, but the less you have to rely upon the middleman the better. In all cases endeavour to make your arrangements for the sale of the produce as soon as you can estimate the crop, which can usually be done many weeks before the time. Arrange, where practicable, for direct supply as far as possible. Growers who have sufficient energy and perseverance to arrange for a direct supply to hotels, restaurants, clubs, and even some private houses, will in many cases find it advantageous to do so. In this case the small boxes, baskets, and crates as described previously may be employed, and they may also be used to advantage in the case of supplying retailers in small towns; and where this is at all practicable, it is better to adopt such a plan than trust to sending large quantities at all times to London. As the result of concentrating such enormous consignments to London in plentiful seasons, good fruit can frequently be purchased in the streets of that city at a much lower rate than it can be bought in many of our provincial towns within a short distance of the growers. Therefore the question of the most suitable market to which to send the fruit requires careful consideration, in order to avoid waste of capital, inadequate profits, and loss or deterioration in the food supply of the people.

In the case of a number of small growers residing in the same district, much might be done to mutual advantage by co-operation in the matter of distribution, not only as to conveyance, but in finding and arranging for the supply of the best markets.

There are three methods of transit adopted—road, rail, and water. The *Road*, where it is practicable, is undoubtedly the best, possessing the advantages of delivery direct from the garden or orchard to the salesman, dealer, or consumer, in the freshest possible condition. Another advantage in thus sending in cases, where large quantities are grown and heavy vans are employed in the delivery, is the usual practice of loading back with manure, which is always required by the grower, and is usually obtained very cheaply in the neighbourhood of delivery; also empty baskets, punnets, and cases are brought back by the vans. But besides this delivery of large quantities in heavy vans, much more might be done than is at present the case, in the delivery to consumers or retailers by light vans. This is especially the case in provincial towns, where an enterprising grower, willing to take the trouble, may send regularly to customers supplies of fruit, over a lengthened period; and in some cases this may be combined with other produce of the farm or garden, such as eggs, poultry, butter, and vegetables. Consumers would gladly avail themselves of such regular supplies fresh from the grower, and growers would reap the benefit in securing the best prices.

Water.—There being only a very limited number of growers so situated as to have an opportunity of using this mode of conveyance, it may be dismissed with only a few words. Even where it exists, it is seldom available for soft and perishable fruits. Some of the Kent growers living contiguous to the river have tried it; and although it is less costly than either road or rail, it was found to be too slow, and occasionally caused considerable loss by arriving too late for intended markets.

Rail.—Hence the great bulk of fruit sent to market at a distance of more than a few miles from the place of production is conveyed by rail. Much fruit is sent in this way long distances, from south to north and north to south, according to times and seasons; and it is a painful fact that much fruit is deteriorated in quality and value through being crowded in transit in unsuitable railway trucks, which have no proper ventilation. The weather being frequently hot at the time, fermentation rapidly sets in, and the fruit is quickly affected.

This not only concerns the grower, in the price realized for the fruit, but the consumers receive it in a deteriorated and unwholesome condition.

I had the opportunity to note the marked difference in the keeping of fruit in different temperatures, when assisting to carry out some experiments on behalf of the Royal Horticultural Society, as to the time that fruit could be preserved fresh in cold storage. We found that such perishable fruits as strawberries and cherries could be preserved fresh and sound for several weeks in a uniformly low temperature, the nearer to freezing point, without being quite so, the better. Therefore, if railway companies could be induced to provide trucks constructed with a cold air chamber, it would be a great advantage, and growers would not mind paying a trifle higher charge to ensure choice fruit being conveyed in prime condition.

Here again we may learn from the Americans, for they have vans thus constructed, and these make up their fruit trains. These trains bring ripe and luscious fruit from the Southern States and California, hundreds, and even thousands, of miles, in fresh and sound condition, to the Eastern States. We want similar arrangements in this country to convey strawberries and other ripe fruit from the southern counties to the northern towns; and when the strawberries are over in the south, to convey late strawberries from Scotland to London and other southern towns.

CHAPTER X.

STORING, PRESERVING, ETC.

The term "storing" only applies to such hardy fruits as will keep in their natural condition for varying periods after gathering, until fit for use, and applies practically only to apples and pears, with the exception, of course, of nuts.

Apples.—There are many varieties of these that will keep in a good sound condition for many months under favourable conditions, and that apples thus preserved usually command a much higher price is well known. By providing the means of thus prolonging the season of supply the grower is enabled to a large extent to choose his time for marketing, and those sorts that can be held until spring in good condition are readily purchased at far higher prices, and when they can be kept until the American supply has become exhausted they realize high figures. Hence it is highly desirable that, where late apples are grown, some proper means should be provided for keeping them until they arrive at their best value.

What are the conditions required, and how they may be provided, I will now try to explain. The first condition is, that they should be inaccessible to frost, except it be occasionally two or three degrees. Secondly, the

Fig. 18.—Apple Store.

temperature should be maintained as equable as possible, and not exposed to any sudden rise or fall. Thirdly, they should not be too dry. Fourthly, some means of ventilation should be provided when required.

The easiest and cheapest mode of accommodation must of course depend upon the resources that each grower has at hand; but the needful conditions are more easily and cheaply provided than many imagine. A cave in a chalk bank or a sand-hill makes an admirable apple store, where all the requirements are present except fitting up the needful shelves. Where this is impracticable, it is sometimes the case that a barn or other farm building may be easily converted into a suitable store by the construction of an inside lining of match-boarding, the intermediate space being filled up with sawdust, straw, or sedge hay.

Where, however, none of these means exist, a simple store may be made as follows. It is best explained by the illustration (Fig. 18.) Mark out the ground for the building, 10 ft. wide, and length according to requirements. Then excavate the soil to a depth of 18 in. or 2 ft., according to the means of thorough drainage. Next build a wall $4\frac{1}{2}$ in. thick and 4 ft. high from the excavated level on either side, and use the surplus soil to form a solid bank at the outsides to the top of the wall as shown. Then form the roof of rafters, which may be made simply of rough poles, and cover the whole with a thick coat of thatch, at least 15 or 18 in. through, and coming down well over the banks at each side. It then only remains to fit up the inside with four shelves on each side, 3 ft. in width, and leaving 3 ft. for the path. These may be formed of any rough boarding, sawn to about 3 or 4 in. wide, and placed with 1 in. space between each, with a ledge 6 in. high in front to keep the fruit from rolling off. A double door should be fitted at one end, and a double window at the other, which should also have a shutter to exclude the light. Leave the earthen floor, which ensures sufficient moisture to keep the fruit plump. The apples may be placed in layers four or five fruits thick.

In such a structure, with shelves 3 ft. wide, a bushel of fruit will occupy about 2 ft. length of shelf; so that a building so constructed, if 100 ft. long, would take 400 bushels of apples.

When placing the fruit in the store, be sure that it is dry, and free from damaged and diseased fruits, and fully ripe. When once placed, it is best to handle or disturb the apples as little as possible. In attempting to remove decayed fruit, it is frequently the case that more harm than good is done.

Some of the varieties most suitable for storing are Wellington, Norfolk Beefing, Claygate Pearmain, Winter Pearmain or Duck's Bill, Mannington's, Sturmer, Alfriston, Ross Nonpareil, and Prince Albert.

For the first week or two they throw off considerable moisture. Therefore immediately after placing in the store plenty of ventilation should be given until the fruit ceases to perspire. After this they may be kept close, occasionally giving them a little ventilation.

Fumigating.—After the store has been once used, be very careful before storing to thoroughly cleanse every crevice. Also fumigate it thoroughly by burning sulphur in it while closed up. This fumigating, if properly done, will destroy all insects and larvæ, as well as fungoid germs. A coating of lime-wash will also help to sweeten the store.

Pears.—These require quite different treatment from apples, inasmuch as they would, if placed in the low moist temperature suited to apples, lose their flavour entirely. Therefore they require a much drier building, and, if possible, one where the temperature can be artificially raised by hot-water pipes or other means. Pears must not be laid so thickly on the shelves as apples, neither can they be kept so long. There are few varieties that pay for storing at all. The following are some that cannot be used when gathered, and may be stored with advantage for a time:—

Doyenne du Comice, Beurre Diel, Duchesse d'Angoulême, Buerre Rance, Chaumontel, Catillac, Easter Beurre.

PRESERVING.

Under this heading are included not only the making of jams, jellies, syrups, and other sugar preserves, but also bottling, canning, evaporating, candying, and other means of preserving. Most of this preserving is done at factories, as it requires considerable machinery and many appliances to perform the work properly, and it is therefore generally treated as a distinct branch. There are a few large growers, however, who have their own factories in conjunction with their plantations; but most of the factories are conducted either by private firms, or by companies, who erect them in the neighbourhood where the fruit is grown, and contract with growers to take all their produce at fixed prices.

I think that much more may be done by growers themselves than has hitherto been the case in preserving some, at any rate, of their own produce. It would not pay to erect costly machinery, or appliances for jam-making, where the growth was only limited. But there are other means of preserving without the use of sugar, as mentioned above, some of which can be effected almost as well by the growers themselves as at large factories, and there is no doubt room for unlimited extension in this direction, as it should be borne in mind that fruit which is preserved without the agency of sugar could be used for a greater variety of domestic purposes, and in much larger quantities. Moreover, any such means of preserving, especially in seasons of abundant crops, would be of great advantage to the grower, saving him from the great loss of having to place his fruit upon the market when it is already congested, and when under such circumstances it sometimes happens that the price realized is sufficient to little more than cover the cost of carriage and salesman's expenses.

JAM-MAKING.

This being a distinct art and craft, it is beyond the scope of this work to describe the various processes in detail, therefore a mere outline will be given. The work commences with gooseberries, followed by strawberries, currants and raspberries, then ripe gooseberries, and

FIG. 19.—STEAM PAN

FIG. 20.—TILTING PAN.

lastly plums. It is, of course, the case that large quantities are ready at one time, and have to be dealt with as gathered. This is a busy time for the factories, and it is an impossibility to complete the process of jam-making with the whole of the fruit as fast as it arrives. Therefore a large portion of it is "rendered," or simply boiled and placed immediately while hot in large stone jars corked tightly and stacked away, to be dealt with as time will allow.

The boiling is done in copper preserving pans, as shown in Figs. 19 and 20, which are heated by steam forced into the jacket of the pan as shown in engraving, each pan being swung on a pivot to facilitate emptying. An enormous quantity of fruit can be rendered in the course of a day by the use of these pans.

The fruit is sorted over and picked as soon as it arrives at the factory, and this picking of stalks and eyes, etc., is performed principally by women and girls, but in some cases ingenious machines are also used for the purpose.

The various processes of manufacturing the jams and jellies, etc., are then performed at leisure, with the fruits, either distinct or mixed according to requirements; and some factories also, to fill up the time during the slack season, make syrups, fruit comfits, and sweets.

BOTTLING.

The bottling of fruit in hot water is one of the simplest means of preserving, and plums, gooseberries, black currants, sometimes red currants and raspberries, preserved in this way are most useful and marketable.

The mode of operation is so simple, and the appliances required are so few, that it is within the compass of many moderate-sized growers to perform the work themselves.

A shallow galvanized boiling tank is required. The fruit is carefully picked and put into bottles, these being then placed together, with hay between and under them, in the tank. The tank is then filled with water to the necks of the bottles. The water is then heated until the fruit shows signs of cracking, when the bottles are filled with boiling water and immediately covered with some air-tight stopping whilst boiling hot. In large factories they are usually heated by steam. The corks are afterwards tied on, and should be covered with a piece of tinfoil, and a neat label to each bottle finishes the operation.

Gooseberries are usually bottled green, and currants when ripe. Plums should be gathered before they are quite ripe, as in the case of some varieties, if allowed to become fully ripe, the skin is apt to crack.

Another mode of bottling has also lately been adopted, by which the fruit is simply placed in the bottles, a liquid poured over them and the bottles corked, without being heated. The preparation of the liquid is at present a trade secret, so that it cannot be given here.

EVAPORATING.

This is a means of preserving that promises to become of considerable importance to all growers. The practice of fruit evaporation in America and on the Continent has during the last few years increased enormously. In years of plenty, when fruit is low in price, any means of preserving and converting it into a marketable commodity must be of value to the grower, and also a benefit to the community. The use of the evaporator is therefore worth a more extended trial, as by its use the fruit is not only preserved from waste, but its use is extended over a lengthened period.

In some figures given in the Royal Agricultural Society's Journal for 1890, it is stated that in the State of California alone, during 1888, the total weight of fruit evaporated amounted to 31,450,000 lbs., of the value of £431,590. There are several different makes of apparatus in use, but Fig. 21 is the one that was awarded the prize at the contest at the Royal Agricultural Society's Jubilee Show at Windsor, and is now in operation at Chiswick, at the Royal Horticultural Society's

Gardens. The following description of the process, and of the chemical change produced in the fruit, is taken from a paper read by Mr. E. W. Badger to a meeting of the Royal Horticultural Society in August, 1890, and is reported fully in that Society's Journal, vol. xii. :—

"It is necessary to point out that evaporated fruit must

FIG. 21.—FRUIT EVAPORATOR.

not be confounded with sun-dried or kiln-dried fruit; the latter are both very inferior in quality, and are in a different chemical state. Sun-drying is still much used in California and elsewhere, but is being rapidly superseded by the more scientific process of evaporation. The description of the chemistry of this process which I am about to submit to you I have selected as being the best

I am acquainted with, for which I am indebted to an eminent American scientist, Dr. J. F. Symons, of Fayetteville, Arkansas. It is the account he gave to the 'South-West Association of Fruit and Vegetable Evaporators' at Springfield, Mo., and will, I hope, afford useful information as to the reasons why properly evaporated fruits are superior to those which are sun-dried or kiln-dried. Dr. Symons says :—

"'I will now describe the process of *true evaporation*. It has been found that by removing a part of the water rapidly, in swift-moving currents of air, heated from 240° F., a different product is the result, wholly unlike either the fresh or sun-dried fruit, which will keep better, is more digestible and nutritious, is less acid, and will sell for more in the market. But if, after having heated the air hot enough, there is not sufficient circulation, or the currents are not rapid enough, the fruit will cook and then dry, or burn the same as in a close oven. Apples will cook in boiling water at a temperature of only 212° F., or bake in an oven at 225° F.; but if the heated air circulates fast enough, the fruit will not cook or burn or become itself heated to the temperature indicated by the thermometer, even at 300° F., for the evaporation of the water is a cooling process, and every particle of vapour leaving the minute cells which contained it carries with it also a large amount of caloric in a latent form, and thus keeps the heat of the apples far below the surrounding air. The chemical changes which belong to truly evaporated fruit will now begin, and the albumen, instead of being slowly dried, is coagulated precisely the same as in an egg when boiled. The soluble starch existing in all the fruit, and composed of $C_6H_{10}O_5$, will, if the heat is high enough, combine with one equivalent of water

(H_2O), so that now we have an entirely different compound, to wit, glucose, or fruit sugar, which will assist in the preservation of the fruit, instead of being liable to decomposition as the dried starch is in sun-dried or slowly dried products.

"'All the pectine, or fruit jelly, remains in the cells undecomposed, or is left upon the surface by the evaporation of the water in which it was dissolved, and may be seen condensed upon the surface, instead of being decomposed, and passing on with the starch and gluten into the acetic fermentation. The diastase or saccharine ferment contained in all fruit, and which is the primary cause of its decay, has been rendered inoperative, and all germs of animal or vegetable life have been destroyed by the high heat. It is by this chemical change which I have briefly described, in uniting a part of the water already contained in the fruit with the fruit starch, that these *truly* evaporated products are rendered more wholesome, more digestible, more indestructible, and are thereby made more valuable, not only as articles of food, but because they are not subject to deterioration and loss. And it is also the reason why a bushel of apples will make more pounds of evaporated fruit than can be made by sun-drying it, as a portion of the contained water which would otherwise be lost is retained by combining with the starch to form glucose, and the carbonic acid, which is always lost in the slow decomposition resulting from sun-drying, is retained in its natural combination with the other substances composing the fruit, and hence it is heavier. These profitable and healthful chemical changes which I have mentioned are all in accordance with the laws of nature, and are certain to take place if the necessary conditions of heat and air, as I have detailed them, are properly supplied; otherwise you will have a different product, and no matter how fine your apples, how perfect your paring, coring, and trimming, or how white you may have bleached them, you have not made truly evaporated fruit, and no matter how many have been deceived by its bright colour, or full weight, or fancy packing, your fruit will not stand the test of long keeping in warm, damp weather. The natural starch, gluten, and albumen of the fruit, instead of being cured, or made indestructible by the chemical changes which constitute the difference between the evaporated and dried fruits, will absorb moisture from the air, will swell or increase in bulk, and be attacked by mould, will absorb additional oxygen, and finally sour and decay.'

"The mode of preparing apples for drying in an evaporator is, first, to pare them, then to remove the core, and finally to cut them into slices or rings. It is customary now to submit the pared apple before slicing to the fumes of sulphur, which process is called 'bleaching,' the object being to prevent the discoloration of the fruit, which is nearly certain to take place unless the fruit is placed in the heated evaporator directly it is cut. The bleaching process is said to improve the appearance of the fruit, and not to injure its flavour. Paring, coring, and slicing are done very rapidly by ingenious machines which are to be bought at a moderate price. The prepared fruit is then placed on wire trays, made to fit inside the drying-chamber of the evaporator, and there remains until the whole of the moisture has been abstracted. The time occupied in doing this varies from $2\frac{1}{2}$ hours to 4 or even 5 hours, according to the kind of apples operated upon. After passing through the evaporator, the next thing is to pack the dried fruit in neat boxes which hold

25, 50, or 75 lbs. These boxes are lined with paper: 50 lb. boxes are those mostly used. They are 24 inches long, 12 inches deep, and 12 inches wide; they are made of ½-inch stuff (with ends 1 inch), poplar wood being preferred. The evaporated fruit, before being used for making pies, tarts, compotes, etc., is soaked in water for a sufficient length of time to swell to nearly its normal bulk."

PRUNE DRYING.

The process of prune drying in France varies from this somewhat, and may be interesting to some readers. It is as follows:—

All the apparatus required consists of trays and two or more ovens. The trays are made either of wicker-work or wood, are round or triangular, and deep enough to carry a single layer of plums, and allow of their being placed upon each other without crushing the fruit. Every morning the trees are looked over, and the fruit that is ripe is picked, just before the flesh begins to soften. The plums are placed in the trays, put for an hour or two in the sun, or in a current of air, and then laid on the floor of the oven. These ovens are made just like ordinary bread ovens; they are usually built in pairs, each one about ten feet long and four feet wide inside, and are heated by burning a certain quantity of wood inside them. When the fruit is put in, the temperature should be about 100 degrees Fahrenheit. In the course of a few hours the plums assume a curious, puffy appearance, and if the heat is too great, they will burst, a result most carefully to be avoided. They are taken out of the oven, cooled, and again put in with temperature at about 132 degrees; again withdrawn and cooled, and this time the fruit is turned by placing an empty tray upside-down over a full one, and turning them over together. They are again put in the oven, this time the heat being raised to 170 degrees. This operation is repeated until all the plums are completely preserved. Some dry more quickly than others, and are picked out and placed in other trays as they are ready. The more slowly the whole operation is performed the better, and the oftener the plums are put into the oven, the higher the quality of the produce. When ready, the plums are sorted into various grades.

The total crop of plums in France, according to *La Nature*, is estimated at 38,000 tons, fully half of this being made into prunes.

CONVERTING FRUIT INTO VARIOUS DRINKS.

Cider and perry making is an old practice in the country, and thousands of acres of apple orchards were planted for the purpose of growing fruit for cider only, special varieties being grown for that purpose, and many of the small farm orchards were cultivated, or more properly speaking existed, for the purpose of supplying the cellar with the required quantity of liquor for the farm hands.

FIG. 22.
PULPING OR STRAINING MACHINE.

But the rapid spread of temperance principles, and the change in the social conditions of the people, have largely altered the old arrangements of supplying drink to labourers, and hence the practice of cider-making by farmers has largely declined. But there is still a large quantity made for sale in some of the old cider-making districts of Devon, Hereford, Gloucester, and Wilts.

But with the decline of cider-making another industry has sprung up in its place, that of the manufacture of

Fig. 23.—Fruit Press.

non-alcoholic drinks and syrups. For this purpose much of the small fruit is used that is sorted out from the finer samples selected for dessert, and these, by the use of a pulping machine and a press, may be rendered into juice on the spot, and disposed of to the manufacturers for the completing processes of conversion into the various required commodities. A useful pulping and straining machine, shown in Fig. 22, is used for extracting pips, stalks, stones, etc., from plums, currants, strawberries, raspberries, apples, and other fruits; and also a useful press for extracting the juice, Fig. 23.

A few contrivances of this kind would enable growers to make the most of their produce and prevent the waste of any.

CHAPTER XI.
GRAFTING, BUDDING, AND STOCKS.

MOST fruit-growers purchase their trees already worked from nurserymen, who of course devote their whole time to the work, and systematically raise the trees for the different purposes required, and the constant oversight required can be better given in the regular routine of a nursery than by private growers. Also, most growers cannot wait the time required to produce the trees of a planting size.

But in some cases growers may prefer to raise some of their own trees, and I will now describe the various operations in doing so.

Apples, pears, plums, and cherries are raised either by grafting or budding. There has, however, lately sprung up a controversy respecting the system of propagating by grafting, and the practice has been severely condemned; but there is no other means of propagation with which I am acquainted that answers the requirements. It is true that some apples can be raised from cuttings, but it is a slow process, and a poor stunted appearance such bushes

H

present, and it is impossible to make a decent standard tree from cuttings. Therefore, until some more satisfactory means can be discovered, grafting and budding will continue. If grafting is properly performed, and suitable stocks are used, no evil results will follow, but far otherwise. Indeed, by the proper selection of stocks upon which to work the different varieties, the cultivator

Fig. 24.—Crab Stock.　　Fig. 25.—English Paradise Stock.

is enabled to exercise control over the general habits of the plant, its fruiting qualities, periods of fruitfulness, and the quality of the fruit itself. This is a matter that has received much careful study during the last few years, and we have probably yet much to learn in this direction. Almost a revolution has been effected in apple culture, for instance, by the use of the paradise stock for dwarf trees, and the quince stock for pears. Both of these stocks so influence the tree that varieties worked upon them commence fruiting several years earlier than the same varieties worked upon the ordinary or free stock. The following are a few outline facts respecting the various stocks used, the purposes for which they are employed, and the influence exercised.

CRAB AND SEEDLING APPLE (Fig. 24). — Used for all trees intended for standards for orchards, or for bush or pyramids of the free-fruiting and weak-growing varieties.

DOUCIN OR BROAD-LEAVED PARADISE.—This stock is more surface rooting than the crab, but almost as rank in growth, and is therefore not of sufficient influence as a dwarfing stock.

ENGLISH PARADISE (Fig. 25).—Used for most varieties of apples for bush culture. The growth of wood is much shorter and closer upon this stock than upon the crab, and with most varieties fruit is produced the second year after grafting, and one of the most important characteristics of this stock is that it produces a mass of fibrous roots which spread horizontally over the surface instead of penetrating so deeply into the subsoil, as in the case of the crab, as shown by the illustrations.

FRENCH PARADISE.—This stock exerts an even more dwarfing influence over the scion than the above, so dwarfing indeed, that it is only suited for the growth of horizontal cordons or very miniature bushes, and for growing in very rich soils.

PEAR STOCK.—Used in all cases for standard orchard trees, and in some cases for pyramids where the soil is very light and dry. The roots penetrate deeply, which in cases of dry soils is an advantage, but on strong lands pyramids make rank growth, and with restrictive pruning become unfruitful.

QUINCE STOCK.—Used in most cases for pyramid and dwarf pears, inducing short growth and early fruitfulness, and like the paradise, it is a surface-rooting stock. Some

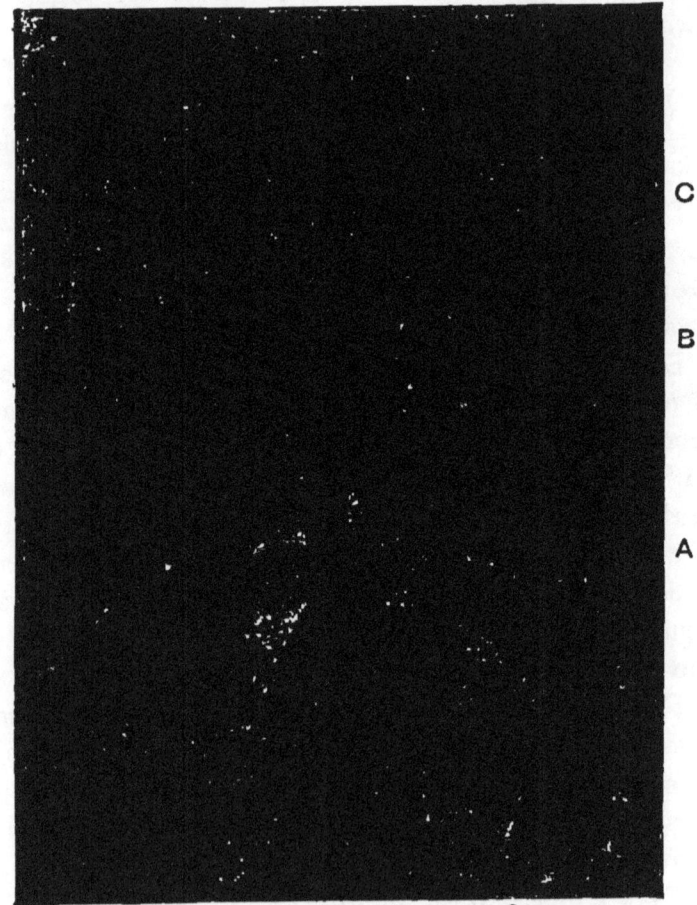

FIG. 26.—DOUBLE-WORKED PEAR ON QUINCE.
A Quince Stock. **B** Beurre d'Amanlis. **C** Marie Louise.

varieties of pears, however, such as Marie Louise, will not unite directly with the quince. In this case they have to be double worked (Fig. 26); that is, the stock is first worked with a variety that takes freely to the quince, such as Beurre d'Amanlis, and the following season a Marie Louise is worked upon the Beurre d'Amanlis as close to the quince as possible, so that when complete there is an intervening piece of Beurre d'Amanlis of only two or three inches in length, but this enables the Marie Louise to establish itself firmly and contentedly upon the stock, and the dwarfing and fructifying influence of the quince is practically the same as if established direct.

In practising this double working it has been noted that a certain influence is exercised over the quality of the fruit, in some cases such influence being for good, so that we have something more to learn in this direction which may be of benefit to cultivators.

MUSSEL PLUM.—Used for plums intended for orchard standards, and also for pyramids. There are two or three distinct types of mussel, which somewhat influence size and fruitfulness of the tree, but not to a large extent. The different types are carefully selected in nurseries, and the free growing and largest leaved varieties used for the standard trees.

MYROBOLAN OR CHERRY PLUM.—This has been considerably used for working plums upon. It is a very strong grower, and produces fine trees in a short time, but it is not very safe to use for strong and heavy lands. Its growth is very late in autumn, and is consequently liable to damage by winter frosts.

COMMON PLUM.—This is a somewhat dwarf plum stock, and is suitable for pyramid or bush trees.

WILD CHERRY OR GEAN.—Used for orchard standards and also for pyramids, being the hardiest and freest stock.

MAHALEB CHERRY.—A somewhat dwarf stock used for

pyramids, and especially for the Morello, which does remarkably well upon this stock.

Preparing the Stocks.—The crab stocks, myrobolan plum, wild cherry, and mahaleb, are all raised from seed; and the quince, paradise, mussel and common plums are usually raised by layering, cuttings or suckers. The stocks are grown in nursery rows until they are large enough to plant out in lines for working. They are then lifted, and the stems carefully trimmed of all side growth near the base, and shortened to about eighteen inches, and all coarse roots carefully trimmed. They are then planted out on well-prepared land in rows two feet six inches apart, and one foot from plant to plant. Stocks thus planted out one autumn will be ready for budding the following July or August, or for grafting in the spring of the following year.

Grafting.—The stocks intended to be grafted are prepared in the early spring by trimming closely any side growth to the height of about six inches from the ground, and cutting off the top at that height.

The scions of the varieties intended for grafting should be cut from the trees in February, labelled and bedded firmly in the soil. This tends to check the flow of sap, and allows the sap in the stock to be more active than the scion at the time of the operation. The wood selected should be clean and free from all disease, of moderate growth, and well ripened. Clay must then be prepared before commencing the work. This is done by selecting good strong clay, and mixing it with finely chopped hay, and cow manure. This must be well mixed, and beaten over two or three times before using.

Grafting wax is also sometimes used, but for young trees worked near the ground I do not think that there is

GRAFTING, BUDDING, AND STOCKS. 103

anything better than clay. In the case of working trees standard high, however, there is some advantage in using wax, as it is less likely to be loosened by motion. It may be purchased, or made as described on page 69.

The time for doing the work is usually March and April, depending upon the season. There are several different kinds of grafting employed, but the one generally adopted for young fruit trees is that of tongue-grafting. The scion is first selected and trimmed to a length of from four to five inches, and always cut close behind a bud, as in Fig. 27. A clean sloping cut is then made at the base. The next operation is to cut the tongue. Then select a clear place on the stock, and make a clean upward cut, as nearly as possible corresponding in size and shape to the cut in the scion. Then from near the top make a downward cutting, forming a tongue on the stock. The next operation is to place the two together, allowing the tongues to pass each other, and press the scion down to the stock, taking care that the two barks unite on one side; then with a piece of bass matting wind firmly round the stock below the graft, and proceed to wind upwards to the top, and finish by passing the end twice

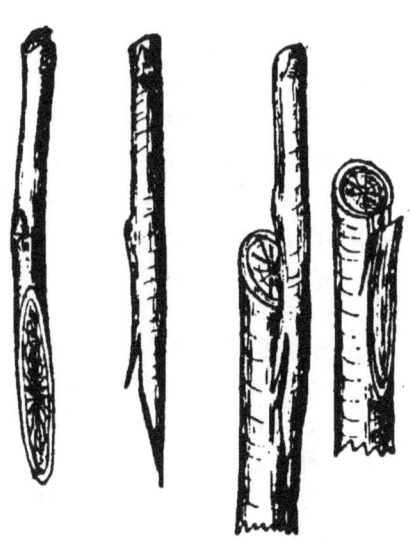

FIG. 27.—TONGUE GRAFTING.

under the tie, and drawing tightly. Then immediately close the wound completely with a piece of clay wrapped firmly round, and press firmly to a tapering point round the scion at the top, and to the stock below. This completes the operation, and nothing more will be required except to watch the clay to see that it is not washed down during rain before the graft has commenced to grow. When the young growth is a few inches high, the clay must be removed, which is done by giving it a sharp tap on one side whilst holding something firmly against the other side. The tie will next require attention, and must be loosened as soon as it shows signs of cutting, which may be seen by the swelling of the bark around and between the bands. As the growth proceeds it may be necessary in some cases to support the graft with a stake, or a high wind may blow it off. The next operation is performed in the autumn, and is called snagging, or trimming off the end of the stock with an upward sloping cut to the scion, considerable practice being required to make a clean cut, and not to damage the scion. A young tree of the desired variety is thus firmly established upon the stock, and may afterwards be pruned and trained into the required form.

Budding is performed at the time when the sap is in full flow, and as soon as the young growth of the tree is sufficiently advanced to allow of the bud being properly removed, this usually being in July or August. The stocks are side-trimmed, but not topped as for grafting. The young wood is then cut from the tree from which it is intended to propagate, and placed in a can of water to keep moist. The branch is next taken, and the leaves trimmed off, leaving only the leaf stalks remaining. The branch is then held in the hand as in

GRAFTING, BUDDING, AND STOCKS. 105

Fig. 28. The buds at the base of the branches and also those near the top are rejected, and only those in the middle portion are used. Holding the wood as shown, make a clean cut with a sharp knife, entering the wood deepest just below the bud. Then come out with a long slope. The next operation is the most delicate and also the most important of the whole performance. Hold the

FIG. 28.—CUTTING OUT A BUD.

bud thus removed firmly by the leaf stalk between the thumb and finger, and with the other thumb nail carefully commence to lift the wood from the bark, then strip clean off by a somewhat sharp jerk. Then examine the bud, and if this operation has been successfully performed there should be no cavity at the bud, but the alburnum or eye of the bud should be left in even with the bark. It sometimes happens with an unskilful workman, or when the wood is not in prime condition, that a splinter of the wood is left below and above the alburnum. In such a case it must be carefully removed without drawing out the alburnum with it. If this should be the case it may be seen at once, as the eye of the bud will have a clear cavity, and on no account should such a bud be inserted, as nothing but the bark is left, and no tree can possibly grow from it.

The bud having been properly prepared (Fig. 29 **A**) is held between the thumb and finger of the left hand, whilst

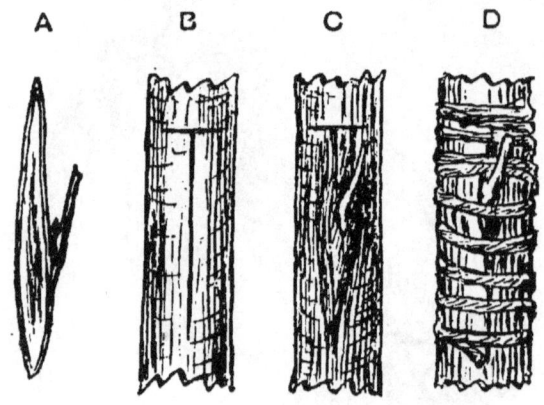

Fig. 29.—BUDDING.

A Bud Prepared. **B** Stock, with Cut made. **C** The Bud Inserted.
D The Finished Operation.

with the right an incision is made in the stock by a clean upward cut, and a cross cut at the top, as per Fig. 29 **B**, raising the bark at either side with the ivory spatula of the knife, commencing from the cross cut at the top. If the stock is in good condition, the bark will rise freely from the wood. The bud is then inserted from the top and pressed somewhat firmly down under the bark, and the upper portion of the bark attached to the bud that still projects above the cross cut is cut off evenly with it, thus allowing it to fit closely to the bark above, as in Fig. 29 C. Then commence to tie below the bud until proceeding upwards you pass carefully, the eye of the bud; draw the tie closely under the point of the bud, continue the band for a turn or two above the cross cut, and finish with a hitch the same as in grafting. If this is properly performed, the bark which was raised from the stem will be drawn tightly over the sheath of the bud, and the bud itself will lie closely on the wood where the sap flows, and will soon form a union with the stock.

No further covering is needed, as in the case of grafts, but the tie will require examining in the course of the next two or three weeks, and gradually loosening as the stock swells, and the tie may be removed altogether before the winter. The buds should thus lie dormant until the following spring. The top growth of the stock is not removed at the time of budding, but is cut off during the ensuing autumn or winter, leaving, however, six or eight inches of growth above the bud. The use of this piece of the stock will be apparent during the following summer, when the bud has commenced its growth, which it usually does at an angle away from the stem. The young shoot is then drawn upright to the stem, as in Fig. 30. This not only gives the young growth the start in an upright position, but secures it against being blown out by wind, which would happen in rough weather and when full of foliage, the point of union not being strong enough to stand the strain during the first season. This portion of the stock, having performed its duty by the ensuing autumn, is then removed at the line A with a clean cut slightly sloping upwards. The young tree is now complete, and can be trained into the desired form.

In budding pears on the quince stock one important point should be noted, and that is to insert the bud as near to the ground as possible, it being most important in planting this tree in its permanent position to cover the whole of the quince stock by the soil, as the stock being very susceptible to the dry weather will, if exposed, cause

Fig. 30.

a check in the swelling of the fruit, and cracking will ensue. The neglect of this point has led to much disappointment and loss, and in many cases has caused the quince stock to be condemned; but if worked close to the ground, and the stock covered as described, there is no danger in this respect. With no other stocks is this the case, and the buds may be inserted at from four to six inches from the ground.

www.ingramcontent.com/pod-product-compliance
Lightning Source LLC
Chambersburg PA
CBHW020830190426
43197CB00037B/1428